To David & Hilary

ty TEACH YOURSELF

PLANNING A WEDDING

with the hope that
this may be helpful.

Much love
Mumsie & Pod / John & Aunt

TEACH YOURSELF

Christine Gillette-Browning

Hodder & Stoughton

A MEMBER OF THE HODDER HEADLINE GROUP

British Library Cataloguing in Publication Data

Gillette-Browning, Christine
 Planning a Wedding
 I. Title
 395.22

ISBN 0 340 64343 9

First published 1995
Impression number   10 9 8   7 6   5 4   3 2   1
Year   1999 1998 1997 1996 1995

Typeset by Transet Limited, Coventry, England.
Printed in Great Britain for Hodder & Stoughton Educational, a division of
Hodder Headline plc, 338 Euston Road, London NW1 3BH by Cox and Wyman Limited,
Reading, Berks.

CONTENTS

— INTRODUCTION —

What is marriage and why, in the face of all the pressures of modern life, does it not only survive but flourish?

Modern marriage, in the many different forms it assumes around the world, is a product of the evolution of humankind. The need to form pair bonds, strong in all creatures, is at its most complex in human beings involving all our senses, instincts, emotions and powers of reasoning, although sometimes the latter seems to desert us, as anyone who has ever been in love will testify! Marriage and the family is the foundation of a stable society, marking the passage from a youthful, self-centred, short-term view of life to the mature long-term, group-centred view.

At its best marriage is a life-long commitment bound by love, loyalty and fidelity, a partnership that sustains two people (and their children, if they have them) through joy and pain, success and failure. It is a public declaration of private promises and the cause of celebration and ceremony.

Most of us achieve a marriage which is somewhere between the two extremes of bliss and misery, sharing times of joy and happiness, frustration and sadness with our partner, knowing that sharing life with someone who cares is a powerful blessing.

How to use this book

We, the author and the publisher, hope that this book will be helpful to everyone who is about to become involved in a wedding, no matter what role they are to play. Primarily, however, it is addressed to those who are, or soon will be, planning a wedding of their own or that of a friend or relative. Generally this will be either the bride-to be, her mother, or both of them together, although, nowadays, prospective bridegrooms are taking an increasingly active role in this traditionally female preserve.

Even at the time of going to press, changes in both civil and Church law are in the making and the once-rigid rules of etiquette surrounding the social aspects of wedding ceremonies are becoming more flexible and in tune with modern society. Almost everyone, whether directly connected or not, will freely offer advice and assistance so, with all the help available, it is easy to understand how so many planners hold the view that arranging a wedding is fairly straightforward. All one needs is a telephone, a telephone directory and a little time, right? Wrong! A wedding is the largest and most expensive event that most people will ever arrange and we have all heard the old proverb about too many cooks. It often proves to be far more complicated than expected, leading to all sorts of strange, and occasionally comic, results.

Arranging a wedding for their respective children, two sets of parents could not agree where the reception was to be held – in the village where the bride's family lived, or just down the road, in the groom's family's village. It was finally, and amicably, agreed that there would be two receptions, one in each village, and guests would move between the two as they wished. This original solution kept the peace. The reception went on for two days and the newly-weds slipped away to start their honeymoon, unnoticed, quite early in the proceedings.

If there is any secret at all in arranging a successful wedding, it lies in careful planning, careful budgeting and taking the time to be thorough. Most weddings take between nine and twelve months to plan, not because a long lead time is strictly necessary, but because most weddings are organised in the chief planner's spare time, with a few minutes here and an hour or so there. Nevertheless, an early start ensures more choice and fewer hurried decisions, even when you employ a professional wedding planner to take all the stress out of the process.

This book takes you through what needs to be done in a logical order. Read through the chapters carefully and you should find that everything is catered for. It may be helpful to record your decisions and actions in the Countdown section of chapter 6 so that you can track what you have done and what is outstanding.

Each chapter takes you one stage further forward in the wedding planning process. Chapter 1 explains the legal aspects of marriage in English law, which applies also in Wales, and the significant differences in Scotland and Northern Ireland. It is not a definitive law text but covers the issues about-to-be-married people need to know.

Chapter 2 is on engagement and looks at how you might like to announce your intention to marry. Chapter 3 is about choices and decisions. It discusses options, and attempts to clear the way through to making those necessary early decisions. Having thought through some of those decisions, chapter 4 looks at how to set the budget and takes you through the planning stage.

Chapter 5 looks in more detail at who does what. Chapter 6 suggests a logical timetable in terms of a countdown to the big day, based on a nine-month planning period. Neither the main topics nor the countdown are cast in stone but can be varied according to individual circumstances, bearing in mind that delaying decisions too long may limit the number of options available.

Chapter 7 covers the wedding day itself, what happens and in what order. Chapter 8 ties up loose ends after the ceremony.

Chapter 9 discusses a few significant aspects of living together as a married couple, such as does the bride need to change her name and what about joint financial planning?

In this book we deal mainly with marriage in the Christian traditions of the Anglican Church of England and Wales and of Northern Ireland and Scotland, the Catholic Church, and civil marriage as set down in the laws of the United Kingdom. The customs of other faiths are often just as complex, and sometimes more so, and it is difficult to do justice to all of them in just one volume. We have, however, included a little information in chapter 7 which we hope will provide a glimpse of some of the many traditions now practised in multi-racial Britain.

It is easy to forget, amidst the excitement of shopping, planning and preparation, that marriage is also a solemn commitment and that the wedding day is just the beginning of a completely different experience and lifestyle. This book is designed to help you with the former without neglecting the deeper implications of the latter. Most of you will read it for the express purpose of using it to help you plan your own wedding, in which case the author, the publisher and everyone else who has had a hand in putting this book together, wish you a long and happy marriage.

It is given that, with delight and tenderness, they may know each other in love and, through the joy of their bodily union, may strengthen the union of their hearts and minds

The Marriage Service
The Alternative Service Book 1980

1

MARRIAGE AND
THE LAW

This chapter deals with the legal aspects of marriage in England and Wales, together with notes on the variations found in Scotland and Ireland and the way the law impacts on faiths other than Christianity. It is not the most exciting of subjects, when you are planning something with all the fizz and bubble of a wedding, but it is vital because, even today, there are some common misconceptions about what is legal and what is simply custom and practice, or vice versa. In this chapter we look at some of the options, explain what must be done to comply with the law, and what can be added by way of celebration and ceremony. If, when you have read the chapter, you are still unsure about anything contact your minister, priest, Citizen's Advice Bureau, registrar or solicitor for help.

The Anglican marriage service says that marriage is 'an honourable estate, instituted of God in the time of man's innocence'. Clearly, then, marriage has a long history and, in most communities, carries the blessings of God (by whatever name the deity is called) as well as that of society in general. In the United Kingdom, the Anglican Church, embodied in the Churches of England and Wales, of Ireland and of Scotland, is the Church of State with the reigning monarch at its head. Because of this unique position, ministers of the Anglican Churches are also registrars and may perform marriage ceremonies that fulfil the legal requirements of the State, integrated into religious custom. In order to have legal validity, marriages celebrated in other faiths and religions must fulfil additional legal requirements.

When the Pope refused to annul the marriage of Henry VIII to his queen, Catherine (of Aragon), Henry took the Church in England out of the Roman Catholic Church and declared himself Head and Defender of the Church in England. He then declared his marriage annulled and promptly married again, to Anne Boleyn. England's Church was, however, still essentially Catholic under Henry; its character becoming Protestant only under the short reign of his son and successor, Edward (and after the interruption of Mary Tudor's reign) under Henry's daughter by Anne Boleyn, Elizabeth I.

What are the legal requirements?

Legal requirements are, actually, quite few. If you are a British citizen living in the United Kingdom you must:

- be legally entitled to marry (*see* p7–9)
- be in possession of certain legal documents (*see* p10)
- live in the district in which you intend to marry (*see* p11)
- give notice to the registrar/priest or minister at the right time (*see* p11)
- provide parental or guardian's consent (applies to 16 to 18-year-olds in England, Wales and Northern Ireland) (*see* p10)
- pay the stated fees (*see* p73)
- either have the banns read (Anglican Church only) or obtain a Superintendent Registrar's Certificate (of No Impediment) (*see* p16)
- have the marriage ceremony performed by an authorised person and registered by a person licensed to do so (a registrar) (*see* p17)
- hold the ceremony in a building licensed for the purpose between the hours of 8 a.m. and 6 p.m. (*see* p9–10)
- make sure there are two independent witnesses, both of whom must be 18 years old or more (in Scotland 16 years old) (*see* p20)

- turn up on the appointed day at the appointed time and give the correct responses (*see* chapter 7)
- make sure you receive one copy of the entry in the register office Book of Marriages (the marriage certificate) which is provided at no extra charge (*see* p137).

Who may marry?

The Christian Churches, both Catholic and Protestant, have traditionally forbidden marriages within certain 'degrees of relationship', which are also enshrined in civil law. Some of these ancient taboos have relaxed a little in modern times but many remain.

Marriages forbidden in law

Most people are aware that they may not marry certain relatives and that these are:

For men	For women
Mother	Father
Grandmother	Grandfather
Daughter	Son
Granddaughter	Grandson
Aunt	Uncle
Niece	Nephew
Sister	Brother

whether the relationship is natural (i.e. a blood relationship) or adoptive. With the explosion in our knowledge of genetics in recent years we are now able to understand why such liaisons between blood relatives are undesirable, although adoptive relationships are also forbidden. This stems from the religious view that a relationship established by adoption was somehow transformed into the real thing by invoking God's blessing. At a time when most adoptions were by blood relatives, when nieces, nephews or grandchildren were adopted by surviving relatives on the death of parents, this made good sense. This same religious doctrine also concluded that, for example, a sister-in-law actually became a 'real' sister because the marriage ceremony transposed husband and wife into, literally, one flesh and one body.

> At one stage in the history of ancient Egypt the heir of the throne (or Pharaoh, if already crowned) was not permitted to marry anyone who was not directly descended from the gods, that is, anyone from outside the blood relations of the royal family, since only a direct descendant of the gods could sit on the throne. This occasionally led to brother marrying sister, or even parent marrying child, because they were the only eligible people available.

It is not possible, in law, for two people who were born in the same gender to marry each other, no matter what has happened since. Consequently a marriage between two homosexuals has no legal validity, even if one of them has undergone gender modifying surgery.

Relationships where marriage may be possible in certain circumstances

Even where there is no blood tie or adoptive relationship, some marriages are possible only if certain conditions are fulfilled. For example, children born in former relationships but raised as siblings in the same family are not, normally, permitted to marry each other. If, however, the new relationship formed by their respective parents began after the elder of the two offspring concerned was over 18, or the children have not actually been raised under the same roof in the same household **and** both are 21 or over the time of their intended marriage, then marriage between them is permitted.

Marriage between a man and his daughter-in-law or mother-in-law, or between a woman and her son-in-law or father-in-law, is possible only if both parties are widowed and over the age of 21; marriage between them when the former marriage of either or both has been dissolved by divorce is not permitted.

These marriages are valid in English law only if both parties are citizens of, and domiciled in, Great Britain or countries where such a marriage is legally valid. If either or both are domiciled in a country where such a marriage is not permitted in law, then neither is it legal in Great Britain, even between British citizens. This could affect British citizens living and domiciled abroad, but living abroad temporarily because of employment may be somewhat different from a legal 'domicile'. The people most likely to be affected by this are those who are still British citizens but who live abroad for most of the year, for example for tax purposes.

If you believe you may be affected by these aspects of the law, but are not sure, check with a solicitor, or the Registrar of Births, Deaths and Marriages. You will find the address in your local telephone directory.

Cousins may marry each other, although they would be wise to consult their GPs for a check on family health records for any contra-indications which may affect their children.

Where and when can you get married?

A religious ceremony may be held anywhere and any time (*see* Jewish, Quaker and Scottish exceptions), but it will be valid in civil law only if it is solemnised between the hours of 8 a.m. and 6p.m. in a properly registered place. Enterprising couples may arrange a religious, or quasi-religious, service whenever and wherever they please and satisfy the law, with a short civil ceremony, at some other time.

Registered places include church buildings of the Churches of England (which includes Wales), Ireland and Scotland, the Catholic Church, Baptist, Methodist, Unitarian, Congregationalist, Free Church, Society of Friends (Quakers), Christian Scientists and United Reform churches, Buddhist and Hindi temples, Muslim mosques, Jewish synagogues and civil Register Offices (i.e. the Registrar of Births, Marriages and Deaths).

On 1 January 1995 the law concerning civil marriages changed and, from 1 April 1995, it will be possible to arrange ceremonies in places other than a register office. Owners and managers of buildings such as hotels, stately homes and castles are now able to apply for a licence which will allow marriage ceremonies to take place on their premises.

There are quite a few restrictions. For example, licences will not be granted to private residences or buildings (public access must be guaranteed), open spaces (parks, sportsfields) where there is a licensed bar in the room (even if a shutter or folding door/walls can be closed) or on mobile premises (ships, boats, aircraft). The building must be deemed 'fit and suitable' and must not 'degenerate the solemn institution of marriage', the designated marriage room in the building may not be used for any other purpose, and the licence fee is not insubstantial.

Nevertheless, there are hundreds of quite spectacular places in the British Isles, and thousands more which are considerably more attractive than most register offices. Once licensing is under way, the options available to couples looking for somewhere 'different' for their wedding will be enormous.

Costs will, of course, reflect the property owner's investment and they are likely to be much higher than current church or register office fees. Enquiries should be made directly to the place of your choice.

There are a few exceptions to time and place limitations. Scottish and Quaker weddings may take place at any time and at any venue; Jewish weddings may take place in any venue and at any time of day, although not on the Sabbath (sunset on Friday to sunset on Saturday) or on certain holy days.

Many other faiths and religions are represented in the United Kingdom today but their places of worship may not be registered, either because they are not officially recognised as religions or their congregations are too small. In such cases a civil ceremony will need to be arranged instead of, or in addition to , a religious service.

Normally a wedding takes place in the parish (for churches) or district (for the registrar) where the bride-to-be lives. If the groom lives in a different parish or district there are one or two extra steps to plan (*see* p000), but the couple may choose in which of the two areas they wish to marry.

On the other hand, if they wish to marry in an entirely different place altogether, one or both of them must establish residential qualifications first, whether the wedding is to be a religious service or a civil ceremony. This means living in the area, for 15 days *before* approaching the minister, priest or registrar to tell him or her of their intention to marry. In the case of a church wedding, the minister will also almost certainly expect them to attend at least one of the three services at which the banns are read, which will be during the three months immediately before the wedding date.

Age, identity, gender and consent

In England, Wales, Scotland and Northern Ireland the minimum age for marrying is 16. In Scotland, people of 16 years and over may marry without parental consent but in England, Wales and Northern

Ireland those between the ages of 16 and 18 must have the written consent of parent(s) or guardian(s).

The couple should each have a birth or adoption certificate, which proves age, identity, gender and nationality, the written consents of parent(s) or guardian(s), if appropriate, and a death certificate or decree absolute if there has been a former marriage.

Details of where to obtain birth and death certificates are given in the Appendix. Enquiries to obtain a duplicate divorce decree absolute should be addressed to the county court at which the hearing was held, or your local county court if you are not sure which one you should apply to.

All requests should be accompanied with as much detail as possible, including full names, all relevant dates, and so on. There is a charge for these services, and they are likely to take several weeks, perhaps even months if details are sketchy, so allow yourself plenty of time.

Baptismal certificates are more difficult to replace. If you do not have one check with your parents or, if that is not possible, ask the minister or priest what to do.

These laws apply to anyone marrying in the United Kingdom, even if they are not citizens. Non-citizens may marry here with either a Common Licence (for a wedding in the Anglican Church) or a Superintendent Registrar's Licence (with Certificate of No Impediment, for a civil marriage ceremony) but not by publishing the banns or Superintendent Registrar's Certificate alone.

— Religious marriage ceremonies —

Marrying in the Church of England

The banns

Reading, or publishing, the banns is the most common route to follow for a church wedding. It means that the minister reads aloud the names of couples who are planning to marry in his or her church and invites members of the congregation to register objections, should they have any. Only serious objections are accepted, for example, if there is a previous marriage which has not been dissolved by death or divorce, or there is a relationship within the forbidden degrees between the parties concerned. Generally the banns will be read at the main service on the three consecutive Sundays that immediately precede the week in which the wedding is to take place.

> The tradition of the banns had a real purpose in times when few people travelled far and most lived and died in the same community as their parents and grandparents. Sexual indiscretions in such circumstances could give rise to a real risk that courting couples may be closely related by blood without them actually knowing about it. Reading the banns obliged anyone with knowledge of this kind to come forward and prevent what would be, in this example case, an incestuous relationship.

Once the banns are read the wedding may go ahead on any day within the next three months but, if postponed for longer, they must be read again. In practical terms, it is unlikely that the minister will perform a wedding ceremony on a Sunday or other holy days since these are the busiest days of the church calendar.

The minister will almost certainly wish to know whether both parties have been baptised and confirmed, so baptismal certificates will be useful. The couple will also be expected to be regular churchgoers and should not have been divorced from a previous partner. A second marriage in church for divorcees is not normally possible although the Anglican Church allows its ministers some discretion and, if the Diocese Bishop agrees, may be willing to go ahead with a church wedding. If the divorced person is the injured party, is a regular churchgoer and would prefer to marry in church, then it is always worth asking because, even though the minister may not consent fully, a church blessing after a civil ceremony may be possible.

Reading the banns is not the only route to a church wedding, although it is the most common. The alternative is to marry under a Superintendent Registrar's Certificate (of No Impediment) although it is quite unusual to do it this way. (*See* pages 15–16, describing register office ceremonies, to find out how to obtain a Superintendent Registrar's Certificate.)

Marrying outside your parish

If the prospective bride and groom live in the same parish, arranging a church wedding is fairly straightforward but an increasingly mobile population is resulting in more couples planning to marry in parishes other than those in which they live. Most frequently, this happens when people leave the parental home, either to study or to work, and then wish to return there to marry.

If one of the parties lives in the parish where the wedding is to take place, and the other lives elsewhere, banns must be read in both. The minister officiating in the parish where the wedding is *not* to take place completes a certificate saying that the banns have been read there and the certificate is taken to the minister in the parish where it *will* take place. The couple is responsible for collecting the certificate and taking it to the officiating minister before the wedding day.

Both ministers will need to see all the relevant documents, that is birth or adoption papers, written permissions and death certificate(s) or divorce decree absolute(s), as appropriate, and both must agree to the arrangement. As before, anticipate that regular attendance at services may be expected in the respective parishes.

If neither of the couple lives in the parish where they wish to marry, at least one of them must establish residency there before approaching the minster to give notice of intent to marry. Attendance at one church service, at least, during this period will be expected as will attendance during at least one of the services at which the banns are read. However, if the chosen parish is the family home of one or both of the couple, and their visits there have been frequent, including attendance at services, the minister may well use some discretion on the point of residency – it is worth asking.

Marrying in the Roman Catholic Church

In the Catholic Church, as in others except the Anglican Church, a wedding is held under a Superintendent Registrar's Certificate (of No Impediment) and not by the reading of banns. The Registrar needs only three months to complete the procedures for issuing the necessary certificate (*see* p16) but a church wedding needs more planning time than this, so it is a good idea to visit the priest as soon as a wedding date has been decided so that it can be booked into the church diary, and apply to the Superintendent Registrar for a certificate later.

Apart from this one item, there is no difference, in legal terms, between a marriage in the Catholic Church and one in an Anglican Church.

Marrying in the Religious Society of Friends (Quakers)

Couples planning to marry apply, in writing, to the Friend's Registration Officer at their monthly meeting six weeks, or longer, before the date on which they wish to marry. A small group of men and women discuss the solemnity of marriage with the couple and then recommend approval if appropriate, to the congregation. The ceremony is held at a normal service, called a meeting, and is very simple. There is no singing, music or special clothes and the couple exchange personal vows using their own words.

A Superintendent Registrar's Certificate (*see* p16) must be obtained in advance. The ceremony can take place at any time of day and anywhere, even in a private house, providing all other legal requirements are met.

Marrying in the Jewish faith

As with the Religious Society of Friends, Jewish marriages may be held anywhere as long as a person licensed to perform and register the event is present and a Superintendent Registrar's Certificate has been obtained (*see* p16).

Jewish weddings are not held on the Sabbath, that is between sunset of Friday and sunset on Saturday, or on certain holy days but, apart from these exceptions, there are no time restrictions – a Jewish wedding can be held at any time of the day of night.

Marrying in other religious faiths

If the church, temple, mosque or meeting place is a registered place, a person licensed to register the marriage is present and a Superintendent Registrar's Certificate has been obtained (*see* p16), then any religious marriage ceremony is acceptable in law. If the place is not licensed and/or there is no licensed person present, then a separate civil ceremony will be required before the marriage is legally valid.

Marrying in a register office or other licensed location

A register office is the district office of the Registrar of Births, Deaths and Marriages, listed in local telephone directories. Each register office has a marriage room where civil wedding ceremonies are performed on any day of the week, generally during normal office hours, and on Saturday mornings. The office will be closed on Saturday afternoons, Sundays and every bank holiday.

Most registrars try to make sure that the marriage room is warm and welcoming although some older buildings can tend to be a little sombre. It should be possible to arrange for pre-recorded music to be played at the ceremony, and for floral decorations to be brought in. The registrar will advise.

The ceremony itself has no religious overtones, is short, quite simple and is, therefore well suited to those who have no religious convictions or who belong to different faiths. For those who have ended a previous marriage in divorce or for those who prefer simplicity to the comparative extravagance of a formal church wedding, it is often the first choice and preferred option.

Notice of intent to marry must be given to the registrar in person and may be made no earlier than 3 months, and no later than 22 days, before the intended date of the wedding. At busy times of the year for weddings, such as late spring or in summer months, it is a good idea to see the registrar as early as possible within the three months. Most registrars will reserve a date and time, if application is made earlier in writing, but the formalities may not be concluded earlier than three months before the proposed date of the wedding.

Application may be made by either, or both parties together, but it must be in person and in the district where the wedding will take place. The same residential rules apply as those for church weddings, that is, one or both parties must reside in the district where the wedding is to take place for at least 15 days before giving notice to the registrar. If they live in different districts, notice must be given in both; the Certificate (of No Impediment) must be collected from the second district and taken to the office where the wedding will take place a day or so before the wedding date.

A birth or adoption certificate will be required by the registrar(s), to prove age, nationality, gender and identity, together with written parental or guardian's consents (for those between the ages of 16 and 18) and proof that any former marriage has ended, such as a divorce decree absolute or a death certificate.

The registrar displays a notice, in the public areas of the office, saying that notice of intent to marry has been received, with the couple's personal details, inviting anyone who knows of any reason why the wedding should not take place to come forward with information. The notice is displayed for 21 days, after which the registrar completes a certificate saying that no objections have been received. The wedding can then go ahead at any time during the next three months, but if it is delayed beyond that date, the process must be repeated.

A Superintendent Registrar's Certificate is also necessary for a religious wedding of any faith, with the sole exception of the Anglican Churches of England and Wales, Scotland and Northern Ireland. It may be used in an Anglican church, in place of reading the banns, although this is quite rare.

Types of licence

Common Licence

Generally, but incorrectly, known as a special licence, a Common Licence is granted by a Diocese Council and permits an Anglican Church wedding without the reading of banns although one or both of the parties concerned must have lived in the parish for at least 15 days.

Application must be made, in person, to the parish minister who submits a request to the Council. There must be a good reason for the request, such an imminent departure overseas. Approval, if granted, is generally given within a day or so and only one clear day is needed between approval and the wedding taking place.

A Common Licence must be obtained if one or both parties is not a British citizen, but is resident here. It must also be obtained by a British citizen who does not normally live here but wishes to marry here. The 15-day residential qualification still applies.

Special Licence

Special Licences are granted only by the Archbishop of Canterbury and then only in very special circumstances. Application must be made in person, preferably at the Archbishop's Faculty Office (the parish minister will advise on procedure) and, once granted, permits marriage according to the rites of the Anglican Church at any time and any venue within the next three months.

Reasons acceptable in granting a Special Licence include the terminal illness of one of the parties linked with confinement in hospital or when neither of the parties is a British citizen and is unable to fulfil the 15-day residential qualifications in the parish.

Superintendent Registrar's Licence

The Superintendent Registrar's Licence has the same purpose in civil marriages, and religious ceremonies other than the Anglican Church, as a Common Licence has in the Anglican Church in that it allows a marriage to go ahead without waiting for the usual 21 days after notice has been given.

Only one notice of intent is needed, even if the parties concerned live in different districts, and either party may give it. It must be given, in person, in the district where the wedding will take place and where one of the parties must have lived for at least 15 days prior to giving notice of intent. There must be a good reason for seeking a Licence, such as imminent departure overseas.

The Superintendent Registrar's Certificate and Licence are issued together and the wedding may take place after one clear day has elapsed rather than the normal 21 days. The Certificate and Licence are valid for three months.

Registrar General's Licence

Introduced in 1970, a Registrar General's Licence is issued only in very exceptional circumstances and is the civil equivalent to the Anglican Church's Special Licence for other religious, and civil, ceremonies. The circumstances in which a Registrar General's Licence is issued is also the same, that is, if one of the parties is seriously ill, unable to leave a hospital bed and unlikely to recover.

The application must be made in person in the district in which the wedding will take place but there are no residential qualifications and no delay once the Licence, and its accompanying Certificate, have been signed. It is valid for three months.

Second and subsequent marriages

In civil law, there is no ceiling on how many times a person may marry. Henry VIII had six wives, although most of us would find his method of ending some of his marriages a little extreme!

Civil law allows a person to remarry if they have been widowed or if a previous marriage has ended in divorce. Church law takes a different view. Both Anglican and Catholic Churches frown on divorce and remarriage, which is understandable when one considers the nature and solemnity of the vows exchanged during a church ceremony.

The Catholic Church does not recognise divorce which is a civil instrument for ending a marriage. Nevertheless, it does allow for annulment, which says that the marriage was not a true marriage from its beginning and is stricken from the record as though it had never been. Reasons must be good, and extremely strong – for example, if the couple married, being unaware that they were related within a forbidden degree. The process of gaining an annulment can take years and the effects are far reaching, for example, any children of the marriage are, technically, illegitimate.

Neither does the Catholic Church recognise civil marriage, since the ceremony conducted in a register office has no religious significance at all.

Since the Catholic Church may not recognise an annulled marriage or a civil ceremony as having been a true marriage, the parties concerned may subsequently seek to marry in church. They must, however, ensure that the Church annulment also constitutes a civil divorce. To contract another marriage in church without completing the legal aspects ending the prior marriage would constitute bigamy as far as civil law is concerned.

Policy in the Anglican Church is broadly the same, although Anglican bishops and ministers are permitted some discretion to exercise their own consciences. Some are sympathetic to requests for second marriages in church, so it is worth asking the local minister for his or her views. Generally they will expect to see that both parties are committed to the church in a tangible way, for example, by attending services regularly and bringing up any children in the same manner. They will also expect to see that little, or no, fault can be attributed to the divorced party for the breakdown of the former marriage. Even then, the minister is still entitled to refuse to perform a church wedding, and is quite within his or her rights to do so.

An increasingly vocal body within the Church of England is pressuring the General Synod (the Church's governing authority) to clarify the situation formally. At present it is possible for divorcees to remarry in some parishes, where there may be a sympathetic minister, but in others, perhaps just a few miles away, that consent may be refused. An early solution seems unlikely but the pressure for change continues.

The law in Scotland

In Scottish law the minimum age of consent for marriage is 16 and, unlike in England, no parental consent is required for 16 to 18 year olds.

All notices of intent to marry must be made to the district registrar, in person, in the district in which the wedding will take place. There are no residential qualifications, that is neither of the parties needs to live in the district, and only 15 clear days' notice is necessary. However, at busy times of year, such as late spring or summer, five to six weeks is advisable. If either party is divorced from a previous partner, at least six weeks' notice is necessary.

The registrar will need to see birth or adoption certificates and proof that any previous marriages have ended, such as divorce decree absolute or death certificate. A Schedule of Marriage will be completed and held by the registrar if the marriage ceremony is to be held at the register office. If it the ceremony is to be in church, the couple takes it to the minister who is to perform the ceremony. A civil ceremony must take place in a register office but a religious ceremony can be held anywhere, providing the minister agrees. In Scottish churches there is no reading of banns.

Young couples eloped to marry in Scotland because the law was much less strict than in England. Gretna Green is the Scottish town closest to the border with England and it became famous as the first place over the border where young runaways could marry without the benefit of clergy or the need to seek parental consent (the age of consent in England and Wales was 21 at that time, but in Scotland, couples were able to marry without parental consent as long as they were 16 or over). Since then, the age of consent in England has been lowered to 18, so there are fewer runaways, but Gretna Green still acts as a magnet for some of the romantic young of England.

After the ceremony, the Schedule is completed with the signatures of two witnesses, both of whom must be 16 or over. The Schedule is kept by the registrar, if the wedding was a civil ceremony, or should be returned to him or her within three days if the ceremony was held in church. He or she then completes a copy of the Register Office Book of Marriages (the marriage certificate) for the newly-weds.

An English Superintendent Registrar's Certificate (of No Impediment) is valid in Scotland, providing the wedding is to be in Scotland and one of the parties lives, and has given notice, there. Alternatively, the party who lives in England can give notice directly to a Scottish district registrar by post, as long as the party living in Scotland has given notice in person. If notice is given in writing, at least six weeks should be allowed for formalities.

If a person living in Scotland plans to marry in England, Scottish registrars will issue, on request, a Certificate (of No Impediment) which is generally valid in England, even though certificates are not normally issued in Scotland. The party living in England should arrange for banns to be read, or apply for a Superintendent Registrar's Certificate, as usual. However, the English minister is not obliged to accept the Scottish Certificate, and may request that the Scottish party fulfils English residency qualifications before accepting the couple's notice of intention.

—— The law in Northern Ireland ——

For marriages in Northern Ireland the procedures are almost exactly the same as those in England and Wales except that the Superintendent Registrar's Certificate is issued after only 7 days, not 21. Every intended marriage must be notified to the District Registrar of Marriages, even if the ceremony is to be held in church.

An English Superintendent Registrar's Certificate is valid in Northern Ireland providing the wedding is to take place there, that one of the parties lives in Northern Ireland and that party has given notice of intent there.

A Superintendent Registrar's Certificate issued in Northern Ireland is valid in England for civil ceremonies and for ceremonies to be held in Nonconformist Churches, Quaker Meeting Places and Jewish Synagogues as long as one of the parties lives, and gives notice in, the district in which he or she lives in England. At the minister's discretion, it may also be accepted for an Anglican Church wedding in the parish where the English party lives, otherwise normal English residential qualifications must be met and the banns read.

Marrying a citizen of a foreign country

Every country has its own laws and traditions on marriage and many are radically different from those with which we are familiar and take for granted.

Domicile, nationality before and after marriage, entitlement to study and to work are all factors which need to be taken into account when planning a marriage to a foreign national. The nationality of children and the status of the foreign national as a parent should also be considered, not only in respect of the couple while they live in the United Kingdom but also of the British subject under the laws of the spouse's country, whether or not they live or visit there. A consultation with a solicitor, and/or a visit to the appropriate embassy or consulate would be well worthwhile. Even when the couple is in full agreement, there is the possibility that problems may arise but, when death or divorce complicates matters further, a little prior thought and planning may save much heartbreak.

Marrying abroad

Going abroad to marry has become fashionable in recent years and several travel companies offer wedding and honeymoon packages to destinations all over the world.

Professional travel companies design their packages to take account of all the legal requirements both in the United Kingdom and in the destinations they recommend, as well as making them as appealing and romantic as possible. It is possible to arrange such trips as independent travellers, but careful checking with appropriate embassies or consulates at home, well in advance, is an absolute must and not for the inexperienced or faint hearted.

The disadvantages of such a trip are that even close family is unlikely to be at the wedding and it can seem a bit lonely, even though getting away from all the fuss seemed like a good idea when the trip was booked. Few, if any, of the destinations currently advertised will have bridal fashions available in the quantity or quality of those found at home and time for shopping will be limited, so suitable outfits, including a bridal gown, will have to travel there and back as well.

The advantages are, however, easy to see; romantic places away from it all, a prearranged, fixed price and an escape from all the family pressures which sometimes threaten to hijack wedding plans at home, can seem very attractive when little sister insists on wearing Doc Marten's under her bridesmaid's dress and the flower girl develops hayfever!

Travel agents are best placed to advise on destinations. There are bound to be many more questions than is usual on a normal package holiday, so a pre-prepared list will come in handy.

Many wedding/honeymoon packages are good value for money but some 1994 newly-weds have reported back that the increasing numbers of couples choosing these options is challenging the capacity of some destinations, making them feel a little as though they were being processed, tarnishing the romance a bit. Your GP will advise on the vaccinations needed and give tips on general health to ensure you both stay fit and well throughout.

The bride does not need a new passport for a wedding and/or honeymoon trip abroad. A woman is not obliged, in law, to change her name to that of her new husband so it is quite acceptable to continue to use an existing passport. It is a good idea to carry the marriage certificate with your passport when abroad, however, in order to avoid any confusion which may arise.

2
THE ENGAGEMENT

He has asked and you have said yes, or maybe it was the other way around. No matter which, you are now engaged to be married. An engagement, or to use an older terminology a betrothal, is made when a proposal of marriage is accepted. It really is as simple as that, and there is no need to make it public unless you wish to do so.

An engagement serves three main purposes; first it is a promise between two people that they will marry each other, second that the relationship is now mutually exclusive, and third it marks the beginning of a period of preparation for marriage. During the exciting months that follow there is much to do and many adjustments to be made; it is a period of discovery and change.

Etiquette says that a suitor should ask the prospective bride's father for his permission to marry her. In sixth century Saxon England it was common for over-eager suitors to kidnap the girls they wished to marry, a short cut which compromised her honour, hastened the marriage and avoided a lengthy courtship or the risk of refusal. Since women were afforded a status almost equal to that of men in Saxon society (uncommon in Europe at this time) this sort of conduct was unacceptable to the majority. King Ethelred outlawed the practice, making it essential for the prospective groom to ask the head of the girl's family for permission. The penalty for failing to obey this law was a 50 shillings fine, a huge sum in those days.

Going public

Most couples will want to share their news and celebrate what is, for them and their families, a momentous occasion. Parents may have been following the romance's progress, especially if the pair still live in their respective family homes or if the prospective groom has followed traditional etiquette and spoken with the bride-to-be's father. Whatever the situation, parents should always be the first to hear that the engagement is official.

Arranged marriages are still common in many societies around the world where parents, and sometimes other relatives as well, decide when and whom their children will marry. The practice has, in the past, been more widespread than it is now, having been the fashion in some parts of Europe, among the aristocracy and royalty, until well into the nineteenth century. Commonality of background, culture, religion, material wealth, age and status in the community are all taken into account and a couple may be betrothed without ever meeting each other. Western sensibilities may be surprised, and even puzzled, by the continuance of such a tradition, having grown used to making personal choices using the more haphazard practice of falling in love, preferred now in their own societies. The success rate of arranged marriages, within the context of those societies which support them, is high. In a society which views love as a bonus, and not a necessity in marriage, friendship and familiarity are stronger bonds.

If there is to be a public announcement, the local newspaper's classified advertisement department will provide publication details and costs. Generally the future bride's parents arrange for announcements, and wording may be along the lines of the following examples:

Smith – Jones

Mr and Mrs John Smith, of Anytown, are pleased to
announce the engagement of their youngest daughter,
Jane, to George Jones, elder son of Mr and Mrs
William Jones of Sometown.

When the parents are separated, or divorced and possibly re-married, the wording should be altered a little to read something like this:

Smith – Jones

Mrs Alice Smith, of Anytown, and Mr John Smith, of
Somewhere, are pleased to announce the engagement
of their youngest daughter, Jane, to George Jones,
elder son of Mrs Janet Wilson, of Sometown and
Mr William Jones of Anywhere.

If one or more of the parents are deceased, the word 'late' is inserted before the name, as follows:

. . . elder son of Mr William Jones and the late
Mrs Janet Jones of . . .

If the bride's mother is deceased, her father may place announcements worded:

Mr John Smith is pleased to announce the engagement
of Jane, the youngest daughter of the late Mrs Alice Smith
and himself to George, elder son of . . .

or ask a female relative, such as the bride's aunt, to take on the mother's role, in which case the announcement may be worded:

Mrs Grace Johnson is pleased to announce the
engagement of her niece, Jane, youngest daughter
of Mr John Smith and the late Mrs Alice Smith
to George . . .

These examples are very formally worded in a traditional way and some newspapers, especially the quality dailies, will stick to their own familiar formats. Even so, there is no reason why a more relaxed style should not be used, if you wish, especially if the bride and groom are arranging their own wedding with little or no help from parents.

Announcement recently seen in one local Midlands' paper:

We've done it at last, so you can all stop nagging!
April Munday and Joe Clark will get married next
May as long as their employers will give them time
off and the bank balance will stand it.

Full addresses can be included, if desired, although it is not common nowadays, mostly because it generates a great deal of 'junk' mail. On the other hand, it is sure to attract a large amount of information on local wedding services in a very short space of time, which may be helpful.

The same wording may be used on printed announcement cards for friends and family who live some distance away. Alternatively, pre-printed cards, which have blank spaces for personal details to be added by hand, are available from any good stationer for around £4 to £5 for a pack of ten. Announcement cards are a good idea for notifying large numbers of people all at the same time, although a personal letter or telephone call is much more friendly.

The ring

As with public announcements, an engagement ring is not obligatory, but it is a well-established tradition which most prospective brides are only too happy to continue! Romantic films often show the hopeful suitor presenting his lady with a gift-wrapped ringbox at a candlelit dinner for two, but it is probably safer to choose the ring together. Most women have a pretty good idea of what sort of ring they would like, so shopping together is far more practical as well as being much more exciting.

Diamonds are the traditional engagement ring stone, but there are many other precious and semi-precious stones to choose from.

As with flowers, there is a language in stones, with each having a different meaning. Here are the meanings of the most commonly used stones, associated with their months of the year.

January – garnet: constancy
February – amethyst: sincerity
March – bloodstone: courage
April – diamond: purity
May – emerald: hope
June – agate, pearl: health
July – carnelian, ruby: passion, fidelity

August – sardonyx: bliss
September – sapphire: wisdom
October – opal: hope
November – topaz: fidelity
December – turquoise: contentment
– lapis lazuli: unselfishness

Second-hand rings are another alternative. Some jewellers specialise in second-hand jewellery and older rings, such as those from the Victorian and Edwardian periods, are often particularly beautiful and strikingly different from the mass-produced designs of today.

Victorian and Edwardian rings often consisted of different stones, the first letters of which spell out a message, for example:

Pearl – Emerald – Amethyst – Carnelian – Emerald = PEACE

Some jewellers will design and make pieces to order, or even reset stones in newly made settings. Your local *Yellow Pages* directory will list specialists in these fields, under 'Jewellers'.

The prospective groom normally pays for his fiancée's ring and she pays for a corresponding gift for him. A piece of personal jewellery is most appropriate, something that he probably would not consider buying for himself such as a signet ring or a special watch.

If cost is an important factor, many jewellers will lend a helping hand. If warned beforehand, generally by the prospective groom, they will be happy to show the bride a range of rings within a specified price bracket and even arrange a payment plan in advance so that formalities on the day of choosing the ring are kept to a minimum. Unless the chosen jeweller has a particularly large range of rings, it would be prudent for the groom to arrange visits to two or three shops, just in case his fiancée has difficulty finding the ring she wants.

For the superstitious, pearls and opals are to be avoided. Both are thought to be unlucky when used in engagement rings, probably because they are 'personal' stones. Genuine pearls are said to develop a deeper lustre when worn in direct contact with the skin, in a necklace for example, but this is not possible in a ring. Opals are said to change colour slightly to reflect the mood of the wearer – too much of a give-away if the prospective bride wants to retain a little mystery!

Party, Party!

An engagement is a wonderful opportunity for a party, a chance for friends and family of the bride and groom to meet, perhaps for the first time. Arranging catering, invitations and entertainment for such an event is a good rehearsal for organising the wedding day. Alternatively, you may prefer a family get-together, a small party for close friends or even just a quiet, romantic dinner for two to mark the occasion.

The 'bottom drawer' is a collection of items the couple will need in their new home, mostly collected by the bride-to-be. Before textile-processing machines were invented, clothing and household linens were spun, woven and finished by hand, which took a long time. To make sure a new home was provided with essential items, young girls would begin to make and decorate linen, and a wedding trousseau, as soon as they were betrothed, and sometimes even earlier, storing finished items in the least commonly used household places, such as the lowest drawer of a large chest, until they were needed.

Whether there is a party or not, friends and relatives will probably send or bring gifts, so it is a good idea to think about where to store them. This is still, traditionally, called a 'bottom drawer' or 'hope chest' even though it may eventually need to be a whole room or more, if friends and relatives are particularly generous. Every gift should be acknowledged, with a personal thank you note, as soon as it is received. It is common courtesy and makes life much easier than leaving all the 'thank yous' for another time.

Closer to the wedding date the groom's friends may arrange a 'stag' night and the bride's friends a 'hen' night. On these occasions friends of the couple take them out for celebration to bid farewell to their single status. Traditionally, stag and hen nights have been different kinds of event, but in our modern society the women's celebrations have become much closer in character to the men's, both groups now generally celebrating with a night out on the town.

> The concept of the 'hen' night is older than most people think, probably dating from the Reformation (King Charles II) and was a get-together of the female members of the bride's family, and friends, to examine the trousseau and contents of the 'bottom drawer' to make sure that everything needed was ready. In Victorian times, when well-bred unmarried girls were shielded from anything remotely sexual, it was also an opportunity for the bride's mother to talk to her daughter about the facts of life.

Nowadays both 'stag' and 'hen' nights tend to be exuberant occasions, generally involving practical jokes and alcohol. With this in mind, it is a good idea to plan them to be held a few days or weeks before the wedding, rather than the night before, so that the prospective bride and groom have time to recover before they play their starring roles to a packed house on the big day.

Breaking up

Everyone loves a lover and an engagement announcement triggers congratulations, attention and the inevitable curiosity as to the date of the wedding. In spite of the happiness surrounding them, some people feel overwhelmed by all the attention and under pressure from the questions and well-intentioned advice that comes their way. An attack of nerves at this stage is quite natural, (after all, marriage is a big step), and generally passes fairly quickly – but what if it does not?

Admitting that an engagement is a mistake takes courage but is infinitely preferable to the alternative. When an engagement is ended, any gifts already received should be returned to the sender with a short note. A long explanation is not necessary, and friends should be sensitive enough not to make matters worse with painful questions. Nevertheless people will, naturally, be curious so it may be prudent to give some sort of explanation, however short and simple, in order to avoid unnecessary speculation, however sympathetic that might be.

If the decision is mutual, each should offer to return any engagement gifts exchanged between them, including the ring(s). If it is her choice, she should offer to return the engagement ring but he is not obliged to return her corresponding gift to him. If he has ended the engagement, the reverse applies.

3

DECIDING WHAT YOU WANT

This chapter is designed to help *you* with the decisions you will be making in the next few weeks and months. You will find that relatives and friends will all want to join in and even, sometimes, complete strangers will volunteer an opinion – have you ever watched what happens in a department store bridalwear section? People stop to stare and often cannot resist the temptation to pass a comment or two. There will be constraints, of course, and most will be financial, but there will be the subtle (and occasionally not so subtle) pressure from family members as well as those of the clock and calendar.

From the day your engagement is announced until the day you walk down the aisle, or step into the register office, well-intentioned help and advice will come your way, whether you want it or not, so how can you ensure that you have the wedding day you want and still keep everyone else, including and especially your parents, happy?

In the following pages we explore the main decisions you need to make in the rough order of priority, with the plus and minus points of each option. There is also some indication of what you can expect to pay for the various options. You might find it useful to refer to the Countdown on page 111, while you read this section.

First, you should decide the time and the place, because almost everything else hinges around them.

——— Setting the date and time ———

Day and date

What should you consider when choosing the date of your wedding? Many couples choose a date which already has some significance for them, such as a birthday, or the anniversary of when they met. Register offices are closed on Saturday afternoons, Sundays and every bank holiday and other religions, such as the Hindu, Buddhist, Muslim and Jewish faiths also have holy days and holidays when marriage services will not be held.

This leaves Saturday (all day in churches, but only Saturday mornings in register offices) and ordinary weekdays of Monday to Friday. Jewish weddings are not held on the Sabbath, which is from sunset on Friday until sunset on Saturday, but may be held on Sunday since this is not a holy day in the Jewish calendar.

The most popular day is, of course Saturday since it is the only day of the week when most people are not working *and* ministers/registrars are available. However, this is beginning to change as working patterns become more flexible and couples discover that some of the services they want on their wedding day are less expensive, or offer more choice, midweek. Providing the guests who are of most importance to the bride and groom can attend, a midweek wedding is something worth considering.

Summer months are the most popular, mainly because the weather is more likely to be good, because travelling is easier (for distant guests) and the photographs will look better. Warmer days also mean lighter clothing and less risk that special outfits will be ruined by rain or that the bride will need thermal underwear! Because the summer months are more popular they may also be more expensive – some providers of wedding services charge more in summer months. Some services, such as transport, may not even be available in winter. Many owners of beautiful, but fragile, vintage and veteran vehicles will not subject them to the ravages of British roads in winter, even for short journeys.

Even allowing for summer's advantages, the number of winter weddings is slowly increasing as people's holiday patterns change. More people now take winter breaks, which is changing attitudes towards taking time off from work in winter. It is more likely that preferred venues, and some other services, will be available at the right time, because demand is lower, hot houses ensure that florists can provide a wide choice of flowers, even in the coldest weather, and wedding gowns especially designed for winter are often stunning, using rich velvets in brilliant, jewel colours and 'fur' trims.

Time of day

Weddings must, in law, be held between 8 a.m. and 6 p.m., Monday to Saturday (excluding holy days). However, there are other considerations which will almost certainly affect the choice of time of day. For example, are guests travelling far? Will they be travelling on dark, wintery roads, which may take longer than at other times of year? Then there is the photographer, who will need about 30 minutes of daylight in which to take pictures. Events such as the local football team playing at home, or the town's street market, can affect traffic and although some events are not easy to predict, for example, whether there will be roadworks in the area, others often can be, with just a little forethought and planning.

The time of the wedding can also have an effect on the budget. For example, if the wedding takes place in the morning, and the reception is planned to go through into the evening, guests will need to be fed twice – lunch (the wedding breakfast) and, most likely, with an evening buffet. For a wedding in the afternoon, however, it would be acceptable to assume that guests had already had lunch before the ceremony and so cater for only one meal in late afternoon or early evening.

The duration of the reception may be affected by the newly-weds departure plans, for example, if they are to leave for their honeymoon on the day of the wedding (many do not, arranging to travel a day or two later, especially if they have booked a package holiday abroad). If they are travelling, and need a few hours to reach their destination on the same day, they may prefer an early ceremony so that they can either enjoy at least part of the reception before they leave, or plan a shorter reception that will end with their departure.

As a rough guide, a marriage service in church generally takes between 40 minutes and an hour, depending on the length and number of hymns and the duration of the minister's address. If communion is included, an extra 10 to 20 minutes should be added, more if it is a large congregation.

After the ceremony, the photographer will need about 30 minutes for photographs, sometimes a little longer if the families are large, or if some of the pictures are to be taken elsewhere, quite usual where churches are located on town or city streets and/or with little space for the photographer to work in.

After the photographs, everyone travels to the reception venue and guests are gradually greeted by their hosts and offered an aperitif and hors d'oeuvres.

Altogether, this amounts to somewhere around two-and-a-half hours from the time of the bride's arrival at the church until the time guests are being seated for the meal.

A civil ceremony at the register office is much simpler than a church service and, since there are no overtones of faith or religion, the issues with which the registrar will be concerned are relevant documents (birth certificates, etc.), the fees and whether the couple wish to add any personal touches to the marriage room, such as flowers or music. The ceremony itself lasts for only a short time, around 10 to 15 minutes, but the duration of all other elements remains more or less the same.

Register offices close at noon on Saturdays, so the latest time for bookings is likely to be around 11.30 a.m.

—————— Church or State? ——————

The image of a traditional, and romantic, white wedding in church is powerful for brides-to-be and for their parents. If both parties are practising members of the local Christian religious community, and neither has been married before, a Church wedding will probably be the first choice. Even those who are not regular churchgoers may still feel that marrying in church is the only proper way to do it.

If you would prefer a church wedding, first look in your local telephone directory *Yellow Pages* under 'Churches' and 'Places of Worship' and find the name of your local church. Call and ask to speak to the minister or priest, and explain that you would like to visit him or her with a view to discussing your wedding. The minister may ask you a number of questions over the telephone, or may just fix an appointment for you, reserving the questions until you meet. Both the bride and groom should go to this meeting.

If the wedding is six months or more in the future, this first meeting with the minister or priest may be a simple introduction, with a further meeting to sort out details, such as music, reading the banns, and so on, planned for a little closer to the day, but it will ensure that the proposed wedding date is firmly in the church diary. The minister/priest will want to be reassured that the prospective bride and groom understand the implications and solemnity of what they are planning, and the Church's view of marriage and its responsibilities. Even the most liberal of clerics will take a dim view of his or her church cast in the role of simply a romantic setting for photographs.

If bride and groom live in different parishes both ministers/priests must be visited. In the parish where banns will be read but the wedding will not take place, a visit may be postponed until closer to the wedding date, around three months before is about right. The same paperwork will be needed, that is, birth certificate and so on, and many of the same questions will be asked in order to fulfil requirements.

The couple will probably be invited to participate in marriage preparation classes and encouraged to join the congregation, that is, attend services and take part in church life generally, if they don't already do so. A Catholic priest may ask about a non-Catholic partner's intentions for the future, to establish whether there is likely to be a conversion and whether any children will be raised in the faith. Each minister/priest is entitled to refuse to marry a couple if they have reason to believe that they couple are not committed to the Church's ideals of marriage.

Preparation classes

'Classes' is a bit of a misnomer really since preparations tend to be informal discussions between the minister/priest and two or three couples at a time. All Churches view marriage as a life-long commitment which carries quite awesome responsibilities and every conscientious minister or priest will be committed to helping couples prepare for their new life together, not for his or her own sake, but for theirs.

Not every minister holds such classes but, where they are held, couples are expected to participate. It is all part of the commitment to, and understanding of, the spiritual aspects of marriage that the clergy hope to see in couples who want to marry in church.

The Anglican Church

Ministers of the Churches of England and Wales, Scotland and Northern Ireland will expect the couple to be baptised members of the Church and attend services regularly, although not, necessarily, at the church where they wish to marry (*see* p12). Preferably neither of the couple should have been married before, unless they have been widowed, and both should be able to demonstrate that they understand the solemnity of the vows they are to take.

The Anglican Church allows its ministers some discretion on marrying divorcees in church and individual ministers may be sympathetic to members of their congregation if they are able to show, quite clearly, that the breakdown of a former marriage was not of their making.

Nonconformist Churches tend to have a more liberal attitude towards divorce, and are more likely to allow a remarriage in church. Even for those who belong to the congregations of other churches, remarriage in a Nonconformist Church is possible if relatives worship there and sponsor the request.

Even so, permission to remarry in church will always be more likely for those who participate in the church life of their community than for those who do not. It is worth remembering that people can be baptised at any age, it is not a ceremony restricted to infants. It is not uncommon for people to begin a commitment to the church through, and because of, a desire to marry there, even though their contact may have been limited or even non-existent before.

If a church wedding is not possible, or if a civil ceremony is the preferred option, the minister may be willing to bless the marriage in a short, religious ceremony afterwards. If you want to have a blessing, ask if it can be arranged.

An Anglican wedding ceremony may include the communion (taking the bread and wine) or not; the choice is up to the couple themselves. If neither, or only one of them is a communicant member of the

Church they may choose not to include the communion since they will not be able to join in.

The Anglican prayer book has been revised and updated twice in its recent history (in 1928 and 1980) and the minister will explain the different versions and which is most commonly used. There may be some flexibility in the format of the service and it may even be possible to add a few personal touches but, on the whole, the service may not be changed in any significant way.

The Catholic Church

A Catholic priest will, like his colleagues in the Anglican Church, expect those who wish to marry in church to be members of his congregation. He will also expect them to have attended services and confession, and be regular communicants. He will not agree to marry divorcees in the church under any circumstances (*see* p19).

The service itself may be a full nuptial mass, or the simpler service which does not include communion, and it is not normally possible to change the order or wording of the service.

If one of the couple is not a Catholic, the priest will also expect him or her to take instruction, probably with the intention of converting to the Catholic faith. If conversion is not an option, he or she will be asked to undertake that any children of the marriage will be raised in the Catholic faith.

If a Catholic is to marry an Anglican in an Anglican church, the priest may be willing to attend the service, with the permission of the Anglican minister and his own bishop, and bless the couple according to Catholic rites. A lot depends on the circumstances but, once upon a time, this possibility would have been unthinkable. In some matters, however, the Anglican and Catholic Churches have grown together a little in recent years.

Nonconformist Churches

This catch-all title covers a wide variety of Churches including:

Methodist	The Church of Jesus Christ and
Baptist	Latter Day Saints (Mormons)

United Reform
Society of Friends (Quakers)
Pentecostal

Episcopalian
Christian Scientist
and others.

Each of these Churches has its own form of wedding service, with a Quaker wedding being the simplest of all (see p132). There is no music, no rings, no sermon or set order of service, no special clothes or flowers and, usually, no bridal attendants or best man. Celebrations of any kind, whether before, during or after the ceremony, are discouraged.

Unlike some of the other Nonconformist Churches, non-members are not normally permitted to marry in the Quaker tradition. If one of the couple is a non-Quaker, marrying a member of the Church, he or she must be sponsored by two adult members of the Society before the couple ask for permission to marry at the meeting house. Because there is no set service, the bridal couple pledge themselves to each other in their own words and in their own time at a normal meeting.

Between the comparatively lavish celebrations of the Catholic and Anglican Churches and the austerity of the Society of Friends, other Churches cover the varying degrees of difference. Some will marry couples who do not belong to their congregations, and some will not, but they all, whether high church or nonconformist, have the same thing in common – a belief that marriage is a solemn and serious commitment made before God, and a blessing and joy to those who make their wedding vows in His name.

The minister/priest will recommend a rehearsal for the ceremony at some stage, although probably not until very close to the wedding day itself. Both sets of parents, all the attendants and the bridal couple should be there so that they may practise their roles. This will help to calm nerves and ensure everyone is as comfortable as possible on the day itself.

Choosing the music, flowers and bells

Music

Wedding music is triumphal, happy and often loud, providing an opportunity for the congregation to give full vent to the celebratory nature of the day. There are dozens of celebratory hymns and anthems suitable for weddings, and the minister/priest and organist will be happy to recommend some. Familiar words and music are best, since guests will be in much better voice with the tunes they know than with those they don't know.

While guests wait for the bride to arrive, the organist will play a selection of musical pieces such as:

- A trumpet minuet by Hollins
- 'Nimrod' from Elgar's *Enigma Variations*
- Pieces from the *Water Music* by Handel
- The 'Grand March' from Verdi's *Aida*
- *The Arrival of the Queen of Sheba* by Handel
- The *Crown Imperial* by Walton
- Selections form Strauss waltzes

As the bride walks up the aisle with her father, the organist may play:

- The first movement from *Sonata Number 3* by Mendelssohn
- The 'Wedding March' from Mozart's *Marriage of Figaro*
- The *Trumpet Voluntary* by Boyce
- *Fanfare* by Purcell
- *The Arrival of the Queen of Sheba* by Handel
- *March of the Prince of Denmark* by Clarke
- The 'Bridal March' from Wagner's *Lohengrin*

There are normally three hymns sung during the service or, perhaps, two hymns and a psalm.

Popular choices are:

- Love Divine all Loves Excelling
- Lord of the Dance
- Praise my Soul, the King of Heaven
- For the Beauty of the Earth
- Now Thank We All, Our God
- All Things Bright and Beautiful
- All Creatures of Our God and King

While the bride and groom are signing the Register, the organist and/or choir generally provide soft and gentle music for guests, or a soloist may sing. Examples are:

- *Air on a G string* by Bach
- *Ave Maria* by Schubert

- 'Minuet' from Handel's *Berenice*
- Theme from the *St Anthony's Chorale* by Brahms

As the bride and groom leave the church together, followed by their guests, the organist will play a short piece which reflects the joy and excitement of the occasion such as:

- The *Pomp and Circumstance March* by Elgar
- 'Wedding March' from *A Midsummer Night's Dream* by Mendelssohn
- 'Toccata' from Widor's *Symphony Number 5*
- *Fanfare* by Whitlock
- *Bridal March* by Hollins

It is a good idea to meet the organist in the church to talk over the selection of music, hearing how it actually sounds in the right setting. An organ played in church sounds very different from a piano at home, so sampling the real thing will be helpful.

The organist and choir leader should know each other and work together so, if the choir is to participate, they can be quite safely left to rehearse and plan together with the minister/priest once they know dates and the order of service.

The organ and choir are not, however, the only musical options available. Some churches have sophisticated sound systems and quite a few are regular venues for other sorts of music ranging from opera to rock to folk. Theatrical agents can provide solo singers, harpists, bands and musicians of all kinds and there may be local amateur performers, who are happy to play and sing at weddings. The minister/priest will often know who they are.

Flowers

Flower arrangements decorate many churches all year round, courtesy of volunteers from the parish. Through the centuries, groups of volunteers and patrons have been responsible for much of the church decoration we tend to take for granted today, things such as tapestries, hassocks, altar cloths and vestments.

Friends of the church will sometimes provide floral decorations for weddings, and often at a more modest cost than commercial florists. It is worth asking the minister/priest if this is a possibility, should the idea appeal.

Churches are often decorated more lavishly than usual at certain times of year, such as harvest festival. If the wedding date coincides, the wedding decorations will benefit without extra costs.

If a commercial florist is to provide all the flowers, she or he will need to visit the church before deciding what shape and size of decorations to recommend.

Bells

Last, but not least, there are the bells. Campanology has many enthusiasts, although some churches do not have a group attached to them and still others have no bells, or just one that is used to ring the services. Here again the minister will be able to advise and a peal of bells, to complete the musical celebration in style, may be arranged if the circumstances are right.

Civil marriage

There are, of course, many people, who have no religious belief or commitment. There are those who have been divorced and those who have a different faith from their intended spouse, making a religious wedding somewhat problematic. For them, and for many others, the first choice will be for a purely civil ceremony.

A wedding at the District Office of the Registrar of Births, Deaths and Marriages is short, simple and has no religious overtones at all but it fulfils every necessary legal requirements. Registrars often go to some lengths to make sure their wedding rooms are attractive and have a good atmosphere. Many of the features of a church wedding can be provided, such as floral decorations, music and singing, although there must be no religious content at all. This means that gospel songs, for example, would not be permitted, but popular love songs probably would.

Most marriage rooms seat around 40 people, some seat more and, while there is no long aisle to walk down and no altar, there will be an avenue between the seats and a table, behind which the officiating registrar stands, and which is generally covered by a cloth and floral decorations. There is unlikely to be an organ, but taped music is allowed (the couple provide this, after consultation with the registrar) as are poetry readings, or other personal touches and even, space and the registrar permitting, live musicians.

Most bridal couples dress more simply for a civil ceremony than for a church wedding, mainly because they feel they should, even though there is no rule that says they must. There is really no reason why the bride should not wear a traditional white gown, or the groom a full morning suit, if they so wish; it really comes down to what 'feels' right.

As more places become licensed for civil ceremonies, conventions on dress will inevitably change to become freer, and the 'white wedding' will no longer be seen as the preserve of church weddings. The scope will be limited only by the imagination and the daring of the participants!

Marrying outside the United Kingdom

Combining a wedding and honeymoon on some tropical, sun-drenched, romantic island, plus having someone else do all the hard work of organisation, has an undeniable appeal to many, and particularly those who have large families who threaten to hijack the proceedings in their enthusiasm.

Travel agents offer an increasingly wide range of packages to places such as the Caribbean Islands, Mauritius, the Maldives, and so on. Travel and accommodation is arranged, as is the paperwork and formalities for the wedding. Travel agents advise as to what documents are needed, both before departure and at the destination.

Most of these trips are for about three weeks' duration, which allows a few days for any necessary residential qualification and for a honeymoon afterwards. Some hotels will move the newly-weds from their pre-wedding accommodation into honeymoon suites at the appropriate time and most packages include a post-ceremony celebration.

Although a three-week stay with all the trimmings can appear to be quite expensive, costs compare favourably with a small, simple wedding plus reception, at home and considerably less than the average of £8,500 (1993/94 figures) for a church wedding in the United Kingdom.

Bearing in mind that the bridal couple still has to provide suitable outfits to wear, carrying them there and back in limited airline baggage allowances, and their friends and family are unlikely to be there to congratulate and celebrate, the foreign trip may suit only a portion of those planning a wedding. Most couples compensate for lack of family at the wedding by having a reception when they return home, although this can push up the final cost to what it would have been if they had married at home.

Reception

Planning the reception is the biggest, single task in arranging a wedding, a task that can spread over a period of several weeks, or even months. The first step, however, is to find a location close to the bride's home and to the church or register office.

Most wedding receptions are held in hotels, largely because a hotel provides space, facilities and staff all in one package. You should always visit hotels twice at least, and preferably three times, before making a commitment; first as a passing customer, to have lunch or

just morning coffee and observe how staff look after their customers. Next, to meet the hotel's function co-ordinator, have a conducted tour and take away the wedding information pack which most hotels provide. The last visit is to drop in to look at the function room dressed for a wedding reception, and the function co-ordinator should be able to arrange this.

A reservation should be made as soon as possible since the most favoured places are frequently booked, for up to a year in advance, for Saturday weddings. Management will want to know roughly for how many guests the reception will cater, and final numbers, menu and wines can be confirmed closer to the wedding date. Each hotel has its own policy, and the function co-ordinator will suggest a date for confirmation of final details.

The menu

Sample menus, a wine list and prices should be included in the hotel's information pack. A good hotel should offer choices of finger or fork buffet dishes, luncheon menus and full three- or five-course dinners with plenty of variety in hot or cold dishes, fish, meat and a good range of vegetarian/vegan alternatives. Check also whether the chef can cope with special diets, for example for diabetics, if appropriate. Most hotels will be happy to build a menu to a client's special request, if asked in advance, and will prepare favourite dishes, produce theme menus and cater specially for children.

Choosing wines is much easier than generally believed, even for those who know little about the subject. Almost every hotel and restaurant uses one white wine and one red, generally chosen by one of the management team, as a house wine. Mostly, these are good quality and reasonably priced. The house wine may be served at table from a decanter, rather than from a bottle, so its pedigree will not be obvious but, as long as it tastes good, this should not matter at all.

Ask the wine waiter or maître d'hôtel not to open bottles of wine until they are needed, then only the wine actually drunk will be billed.

Traditional etiquette says that sherry is served with hors d'oeuvres, fish should be accompanied by white wine and meat, especially game and red meat, by red. Champagne is the drink of celebration and a sweet wine accompanies desserts. There is a good deal of common sense behind these traditions in that a red wine, with a full rich taste, would tend to swamp the delicate flavour of fish and a dry wine will taste tart and sharp against the sweetness of most desserts.

To welcome guests to the reception, the most popular choices are either dry sherry, buck's fizz (a mixture of champagne and fresh orange juice) or champagne, with a fruit juice for those who do not take alcohol. For the meal, a medium white and soft red are safe choices and the hotel's wine waiter or maître d'hôtel may even arrange for a tasting to help with the decision.

There is nothing quite like the taste of a good champagne, especially with a generous helping of caviar! Champagne is, however, quite expensive so, if the budget will not stretch quite that far, try a sparkling white wine instead. There are several very good sparkling white wines available, and again the wine waiter will help with recommendations.

A welcoming drink/aperitif for guests, and wine with the meal, is normally arranged at the same time as, and included in the costs of, the wedding breakfast. Nowadays other drinks are left to the discretion of the guests themselves. The function suite at the hotel will have its own bar, which is generally opened as soon as the meal is finished, and guests buy their own drinks. Sometimes the bride's parents, or the newly-weds themselves, 'put money behind the bar' and the first drinks are served free to guests. A completely 'free' bar is rare these days but the function co-ordinator will arrange it, if asked. The most usual way is for a sum of money to be paid to the hotel in advance, with a fully accounted bar bill being made available to the person concerned after the reception with a refund/additional payment as appropriate.

Special requirements

While discussing arrangements with the function co-ordinator, he or she should be advised of any other needs, such as access for a florist or party decorator (balloons and so on), or if any of the guests are on special diets or need help with wheelchairs. The co-ordinator will also want to know what entertainment has been arranged and whether access to put up equipment is required before the reception begins. Entertainers will also be grateful for a warning if the room has difficult acoustics which might distort sound, the co-ordinator should be able to advise.

Children, especially little ones, can quickly become tired and overexcited, or even bored, at adult functions so, if there will be children present at yours, you might like to consider hiring a clown or a puppet theatre to keep them entertained, or perhaps arrange for a video for them to watch.

Receiving line

If there is to be a formal receiving line, the function co-ordinator should be asked to keep the reception room closed until after the newly-weds, their parents and senior attendants, are ready to receive the guests. This may involve arranging for a member of the hotel staff to guide early guests into a lounge or waiting area for a time and offer them appropriate hospitality and refreshments.

The receiving line is made up of the bride's parents, the groom's parents, the newly-weds and their senior attendants, in that order, starting with the bride's mother closest to the entrance.

Guests →

Receiving Line

Bride's Mother	Bride's Father	Groom's Mother	Groom's Father	Bride	Groom	Chief Brides-maid	Best Man

Top table seating plan

The top table accommodates the bridal party and there are several acceptable seating plans which cope with different situations. The first, and most common, is for nine people with the bride seated in the centre with the groom on her right, her mother on his right, then the groom's father and finally the chief bridesmaid/matron-of-honour. The bride's father sits on the bride's left and next to him sits the groom's mother, the best man and second bridesmaid.

Chief Brides- maid	Groom's Father	Bride's Mother	Groom	Bride	Bride's Father	Groom's Mother	Best Man	Second Brides- maid

Complications might arise in families where both natural and step-parents are present, especially where there is some inter-relationship tension. A family conference several weeks prior to the wedding, if this is possible, may help ensure the wedding day is free from unnecessary difficulties and there are alternative seating plans which may also help to ensure things so smoothly. These alternatives should be discussed with the function co-ordinator when booking the reception.

Step Mother (Groom)	Step Father (Bride)	Chief Brides- maid	Groom's Father	Bride's Mother	Groom	Bride	Bride's Father	Groom's Mother	Best Man	Step Mother (Bride)	Step Father (Groom)

Best Man	Step Mother (Groom)	Groom's Father	Bride's Mother	Groom	Bride	Bride's Father	Groom's Mother	Step Father (Groom)	Chief Brides- maid

The alternative plans seat both step-parents and natural parents at the top table, while putting a little distance between them all. The natural parents are seated in the centre, emphasising their closer relationship and involvement with the couple.

Accommodation

If the bride and groom are to stay at this or any other hotel on their wedding night, their reservation should be made in plenty of time because bridal suites, like function and banqueting rooms, tend to be booked up well in advance. Should a room be needed for children, either for naps, for alternative entertainment or a video show, or if a quiet room is to be provided for guests, reservations for these should be made at the same time.

As guests respond to invitations it may become clear that some plan to stay the night rather than return home after the reception. A little research into hotels and guest houses, for the bride and/or her mother to pass on, will help smooth the way. Alternatively, accommodation might be booked on behalf of guests and the matter will be simplified if this is in the hotel where the reception is to be held.

Other venues

At one end of the spectrum, the reception may be self-catered in a local hall or function room. Don't forget to check about drinks and entertainment licences with the facility owner or manager. There are mid-range hotels and restaurants, and for something a little different, river cruises, stately homes, wineries and vineyards, luxury hotels, theme parks, fun fairs or even Tower Bridge. If the bride's home is large enough, you can even hold the reception there.

At a three-star hotel, expect to pay around £2 per head for reception line drinks, around £40 to £45 for a seated, silver service meal and from £20 for a buffet; wine is extra. A bottle of wine from an off-licence is less expensive than the same bottle at a three-star hotel but, if wine is brought in, the hotel will charge corkage. The costs should include hire of the facility, the loan of linen, crystal and china, table centre decorations, the meal itself, cake stand and slice and waiting staff.

For summer weddings and/or to extend the capacity of hotels and other facilities, marquees, erected and equipped with furniture, catering equipment, heating, lighting, carpeted floors and draped and flounced linings, can be hired from specialist companies. A large private garden, a hotel garden or river bank are ideal sites although permission from the relevant local authorities may be needed if the site is publicly owned.

The cost of a good quality, small marquee, fully equipped, will be around £1,200 to £1,500, depending on location and the kind of fittings needed. A larger size, big enough for 250 people or so, could cost upwards of £4,000. These costs do not include catering, entertainment or a bar, which will need to be provided separately.

Caterers

If the reception is to be held elsewhere than at a hotel, for example, in a school, a function room, marquee or village hall, then a separate caterer will need to be engaged. If the venue has its own kitchen this should be fairly straightforward but, if not, then a caterer with a mobile kitchen will be needed. Most managers of halls and rooms will be able to recommend a caterer and also, most probably, a mobile bar. Check first whether the facility is likely to be granted an alcohol licence and whether it is already licensed for entertainment. Again, the manager or caretaker of the facility will be able to help and, if there is no permanent licence, the caterer and/or bar manager will apply for one to the local courts.

Bringing in a mobile bar should not cost anything if there are likely to be more than 70 to 80 people at the reception, since the owner will make his or her fee from the drinks purchased. Arrangements are the same as for the bar in a hotel, that is, guests may buy all their own drinks, a sum of money to cover the first two or three may be put behind the bar, or the bill may be picked up in its entirety by parents and/or newly-weds. The bar should come complete with optics, beer and spirits, mixers, glasses and so on, although ice may need to be provided from elsewhere. The caterer should be able to help with this, if the bar staff are unable to.

The caterer should be able to provide everything needed, such as crystal, linen, silverware, table decorations, china, serving dishes and so on, not forgetting waiting staff plus a guarantee to clear and clean dishes when the meal is over. Cleaning the room or hall after a function is normally the responsibility of the owners or manager, but sometimes it is classed as an extra and charged accordingly. Check first and make appropriate arrangements.

Ask to see samples of the caterer's work before committing yourself to a booking. The caterer should be able to accommodate a request for a sample of work, either by arranging for a visit to a function being catered for another client or providing sample-sized dishes from the menu.

Attendants

There are no hard and fast rules about the number of attendants suitable for a church wedding but generally the size of the bride's and groom's families, and of the budget, will suggest a likely number.

Anything between one and six bridesmaids is quite usual. Female attendants are usually young, single females from the bride's family. If she has no relatives, or too few to fit the bill, then she will normally choose first from her fiance's family and then from among close friends. The matron-of-honour is almost always either the bride's older, married sister or a very close friend and will normally be the only female attendant.

Girls under the age of eight or so would not normally be expected to be a lone bridesmaid (children are quickly bored when expected to stand around doing nothing except look demure, which can account for quite a lot of time in a bridesmaid's day) and two attendants below this age would be sufficient. Every child attendant under ten should, ideally, be matched with an adult bridesmaid taking care of them while they are 'on duty'.

A flower girl, a pageboy and/or a ring bearer would normally be in addition to the bridesmaids, and adult attendants, especially the chief bridesmaid, are expected to keep an eye on them throughout the day.

Male attendants are the best man and ushers, generally, but not always, in the same numbers as there are adult bridesmaids. Ushers are usually chosen from the among the young, single males of the groom's family. If there are too few male relatives that fit the profile, then some may be chosen from among the groom's circle of close friends and then from the bride's family.

The best man's role, historically, was to make sure the groom didn't get too drunk to get to his wedding, didn't change his mind and thereby disgrace both his family and that of the bride, and wasn't injured in ill-judged escapades too close to the wedding date. Ushers were, and still are to some degree, minders, guardians who made sure that etiquette was maintained at the wedding and that too much high-spirited behaviour didn't spoil the day.

A fairly large wedding might have six bridesmaids (e.g. four adults and two children), a flower girl and a boy ring bearer, the best man and three ushers. The best man partners the senior bridesmaid in the procession out of the church and at the reception, and the other three adult bridesmaids are paired with the ushers, with all eight keeping a close eye on the four children.

Alternatively, the bride may choose to have just one attendant, say a matron-of-honour, who will pair with the best man for the procession and during the reception afterwards.

What to wear

Almost everyone going to a wedding will think long and hard about what to wear. At this point, you do not need to worry about purchasing, but you might like to decide colour schemes, shapes, and so on. This will help you to choose items such as flowers, stationery and cake decorations to co-ordinate.

The bride's dress

The growth in popularity of the white bridal gown began in the mid-nineteenth century when Queen Victoria chose white, instead of the traditional royal silver, for her wedding gown when she married Prince Albert of Saxe-Coburg in 1840.

In ancient Rome the bridal colour was yellow. In Chinese societies, it has traditionally been red, highlighted with green and gold. This combination is thought to promote wealth, health and happiness.

Ready to wear

Shopping for the perfect dress is probably the most exciting part of wedding preliminaries, often involving the bride's mother and the bridesmaids as well as the bride herself. As with every other fashion, bridal gowns have their 'seasons', which begin with international shows in Harrogate and London during the autumn. Designs displayed there will fill the shops from October onwards, with originals selling for several thousands of pounds.

The range of styles and fabrics is immense, with colours from the palest of pale pastels, through ivory and cream to pure, shimmering white. Deeper, jewel colours and tartans, in heavy brocades, ribbons and velvets may be added as trims, or made into capes and jackets for winter brides. Ready-to-wear collections will start at prices from around £300, with made-to-measure and designer styles, especially those made with the more expensive fabrics, embroidery and beadwork, costing from a few hundred to many thousands of pounds.

Many retailers sell off their display stock in January and February and it is possible to find genuine bargains. They need searching out, however, because many bridal retailers don't advertise sales, and gowns with reduced prices are often displayed on rails alongside items still at full price. Most of the display stock offered at reduced prices will have been on the rails for a few weeks, or even months, but the retailer will almost certainly arrange for a dress to be cleaned for a customer, if it guarantees a sale. Bridal shops should also have an alterations capability, generally contracted out to home-based workers. Cleaning and alterations may be charged as extras, over and above the ticket price of the gown. Ask for prices before agreeing to a sale.

Hiring a dress

Wedding gowns can also be hired for the day. Most companies will hire out each wedding dress three or four times, the first hirer will pay around 50 to 60 per cent of the retail value, the second around 30 to 40 per cent and third and fourth about 25 per cent. Hire dresses are often sold at the end of the season, sometimes by the hire company direct and sometimes through dress agencies, which is a good way of acquiring a very expensive dress at a fraction of its original cost.

Dresses for hire are generally of simpler design than their more extravagant ready-to-wear or made-to-measure alternatives because they must be washable or dry cleanable. Much of the machine-made lace and heavy beadwork adorning so many designs nowadays is difficult to clean safely.

Alternative ideas

A traditional bridal gown may not be to everyone's taste and some designers specialise in making outfits that are just a little different. Retailers of evening wear often have suitable outfits, which may have more appeal for older brides, who may feel that traditional styles are a bit 'young' for them, or for those who feel that they would prefer something less elaborate for their second wedding.

To capture the romantic look and feel without the floor length formality there are ballerina and knee length dresses, in the same shades and fabrics as traditional gowns, plus pastel shades of peach, pink and blue.

For a slender figure, sheath styles are extremely flattering and for the bride with a sense of history, there are gowns which reflect the gracious age of Edwardian England or the roaring twenties.

Brides who prefer something a little more conservative might consider the larger bridal retailers who market ranges of suits, and dress and jacket outfits, often made from the same fabrics as bridal gowns.

Made to measure

Ready-to-wear bridal retailers do not, as a rule, hold stock; the dresses on display are for clients to try and then order which can take several weeks, or even months.

Similarly, dressmakers programme their time several months ahead, so early enquiries are essential. If the bride chooses to have an outfit made especially for her, it is important that she has a good relationship with the dressmaker. The dressmaker may be highly experienced and skilful but artistic interpretation on the bride's wishes will be so much easier if they communicate well and are on the same wavelength. It is helpful if you can take a photograph from a magazine, or a sketch you have made yourself, when you start to discuss what you want. Sometimes, especially if you are uncertain about what you want, it is a good idea to try some styles on in a shop first, even if you are planning to have your dress made.

For shopping trips, the companionship of someone whose judgement the bride trusts is invaluable. The final selection belongs, of course, to the bride, but a helping hand and another pair of eyes when reviewing the huge selection of dresses on offer will generally be more than welcome. You may find that you need to try many on before deciding what really suits you and fits in with the style of wedding you are planning.

Accessories

Accessories should always be chosen *after* the dress, never before. Accessories that match and complement the dress are far easier to find than the the other way around and, if need be, shoes can be dyed to match and the headdress made to order.

Larger bridal wear retailers generally stock a whole range of accessories from veils to garters and headdresses to shoes. Shoes should feel comfortable right from the start since the bride is likely to spend most of the wedding day on her feet. Wearing them indoors at every opportunity will break them in before the big day.

Buying

Bear in mind that you may be buying an outfit in February to wear in August, or perhaps the other way around – the weather will be very different when you wear it for real.

Whether the choice is for ready made, hire or made to measure, bridal magazines are the best place to start looking. Every issue contains dozens, sometimes hundreds, of designs, plus information on stockists. *Yellow Pages* is a good source of information for local areas, check 'Ladies Wear, Hire', 'Dressmakers', and 'Wedding Services'.

Having decided what you want, the best time for shopping is around five to six months before the wedding. Too early and there is a risk that something better will come along after the budget has been spent, and a free choice may not be possible. If the dream dress proves to be somewhat illusive in the retail sector, there is still time, at around four to five months before the wedding, to have a dress made.

Going-away outfits

Traditionally, the bride and groom change out of their wedding outfits into something more suitable for travelling, just before leaving the reception to go on their honeymoon, hence the name 'going-away outfit'. Nowadays, fewer couples leave the reception this way – many go on their honeymoon a few days later (largely because holiday charter flights take advantage of off-peak reductions in airport tariffs) or simply stay on at the reception in order to enjoy themselves along-side their guests. If this is the case, the bride will often stay in her wedding dress as long as possible – and who would blame her – changing into a party or cocktail outfit later in the evening. Buying a wedding dress, a party outfit *and* something to go away in later can work out to be quite expensive but there are few reasons as good as one's wedding day for a little self-indulgence!

If the groom is married in a lounge suit, he may feel it will double as his going-away suit as well, but if he has married in a morning suit, a uniform or highland dress, he, too, may splash out on something new for his honeymoon.

Bridesmaids and the matron-of-honour

Bridesmaids are most often dressed in a style and colour that comple-ments the bridal gown. When the bridesmaids are all of similar colouring, age and build this works very well but if not, one alterna-tive is to choose a common style but different colours. This works best when there are several bridesmaids, for example, one pair might wear pale blue, another lavender, and so on.

The bride and her attendants should all be in agreement, which may need a bit of give and take. A red-head, for example, may have very strong opinions on wearing the bride's favourite baby pink, and the elegant Edwardian style she favours may not suit the 6-year-old as well as the 26-year-old.

> The superstitious may wish to avoid any shade of green, even turquoise, since it is said to be unlucky at a wedding.

As with the bridal gown, the dresses may be bought at a ready-to-wear shop, hired for the day or made to measure. Etiquette says that if a dress is suitable for alternative wear, as a ballgown, for example, the bridesmaid should pay for her own dress and keep it after the wedding. If, however, a dress is clearly unsuitable for wearing again, the bride (or her father, if he is the host in a full, traditional, sense) pays and the dress is the bridesmaid's to keep or dispose of.

To hire a bridesmaid's dress costs from around £40 upwards, with made-to-measure and ready-to-wear dresses from around £60. Designer dresses and/or those made from more expensive fabrics can cost quite a bit more.

Hire companies generally carry a wide range of colours although not, necessarily, a wide choice of styles. Dresses should be cleaned or laundered between each hiring, so check necklines, hems, wrists and under arms for tell-tale signs.

Timescales for searching and shopping are about the same as for the bridal gown, but it is prudent to choose the bridal gown before shopping for bridesmaids' outfits.

Children

Small bridesmaids often wear the same style and colour of dress as the adult attendants but, if the adult style is unsuitable for children, dressing them differently is quite acceptable as long as the different outfits complement each other in some way. As with adult styles, little dresses can be bought at ready-to-wear retailers, hired for the day, or made to measure. Prices for hiring start at around £25, and expect to pay from £35 upwards to buy either ready to wear or made to measure. Designer dresses can easily cost several hundreds of pounds, even for small children's dresses.

For page boys and ring bearers, hiring an outfit is by far the best option. Small versions of highland dress, costumes of satin shirts and knee breeches and miniature morning suits are available from menswear hire shops and prices start from around £25.

The main consideration, when choosing outfits for child attendants, is that they will almost certainly wear them for a good part of the day, perhaps from quite early in the morning until the reception ends or they are taken home to bed. Children can be tough on clothes, so hiring may not be the best option since any damage will be charged to the customer. However, if the bride has set her heart on a miniature morning suit, or a Cinderella-style footman's satin suit, the solution may be for children to change out of their hired outfits immediately after the ceremony and before the reception actually begins.

Menswear

What the men wear depends, to a great degree, on the style of wedding. Nowadays many men live and work in casual clothes and some marry in them as well although it is not very common, even in today's relaxed society. Lounge suits are quite acceptable and will repay the investment by being wearable on other occasions.

Morning suits are increasingly popular, with many good menswear shops having a hire section. To hire a complete outfit of trousers, tail coat, cravat, gloves and hat will cost from about £60 upwards, depending on size and quality. Remember that it is usual for the groom, ushers, and best man to wear the same colours and style, except, perhaps, for the cravat and optional waistcoat, where differences can lend a touch of originality to an otherwise uniform look.

Most men's wear for weddings is hired for the occasion nowadays. Since the hire market is quite substantial and widespread, most towns have at least one gentlemen's outfitters that will hold, or have access to, a range of items. Once again, *Yellow Pages* will help to locate them.

Reputable companies will clean a suit each time it is hired but, to be sure, check pockets, turn-ups and under the collar for confetti – if it is there, the chances are that the suit has not been cleaned since it was last worn.

The groom and his attendants should, wherever possible, arrange to hire their suits from the same outfitters, or the same branch if the outfitter is one of a chain or franchise. Different shops stock the work of different tailors, and the shades, colours and styles vary from place to place, even within the same company. Fittings should be arranged, and reservations made, around three months before the wedding.

Alternatives

Members of the armed forces are permitted to wear uniform for their weddings, although few women take up the option for obvious reasons.

During the Second World War many brides wore their uniforms, partly because the rationing of fabrics and clothes allowed little choice and partly because, under the pressures of operational requirements, many marriages were arranged very quickly.

Servicemen, on the other hand, do marry in uniform, often at the request of the prospective bride and both sets of parents. Dress uniforms are out of the ordinary, frequently spectacular to look at, and look wonderful in the photographs. They also have a distinct advantage in that they involve little, or no, extra expenditure!

If the groom is in the services, it is likely that some of the guests and the best man may also be in the services. If so, they would generally be expected to wear uniform. It may even be possible, if they are in the appropriate services and ranks, to arrange a guard of honour, with an archway of drawn swords under which the procession out of the church would pass.

If the groom is a Scot, he may wish to wear full, ceremonial dress in his clan tartan. These can also be hired for the day, although, generally, hire companies supply only the most common tartans. Clan tartans can be bought ready made or to order. There are more companies providing this service in Scotland than in other parts of the United Kingdom, but most will work by mail order, if required.

Transport

'Just get me to the church on time', says the song, and it is true that the transport is what brings everything together on the big day.

A car is the most common form of transport hired for a wedding, but there are many different sorts of car and a wide variety of other forms of transport to choose from. Prices vary a great deal, generally because providers range from the enthusiastic owner/driver, who wants to earn enough to pay for the upkeep of his pride and joy, to nationwide vehicle hire companies.

A white Rolls Royce is always popular, and Rolls Royce and Bentley limousines are probably the most commonly hired wedding cars.

Many vintage and veteran cars are small inside, something to remember if the wedding dress has petticoats, hoops and/or a train. They are more expensive simply because they tend to be fragile and require expensive maintenance and insurance cover to keep them on the road. Many owners will not accept bookings for the winter months, because of the strong possibility of inclement weather. Remember that your hair and veil, at least, will be affected by a trip in an open-topped tourer.

Vintage and veteran cars and horse-drawn carriages are the next most popular, but brides have been taken to the church or register office in motorcycle sidecars, helicopters, boats and every conceivable type of transport there is.

Local papers have advertisements for wedding cars for hire and more can be found in your *Yellow Pages*. If the choice is for a specialist vehicle, such as a vintage Rolls Royce or 'Cinderella's magic coach', it is important to book early because there are not many of them around and it is a case of first come, first served.

Before the ceremony

The bride's transport

The bride's transport is very important, not just because it brings her to the church or register office but because the whole day hinges around its being at the right place at the right time. At certain times of year the church may have more than one wedding booked during the day, and a register office is likely to have several, so a late arrival could threaten the arrangements of more than one family.

Before booking the transport and confirming with a deposit, take a little time to visit the owner, or company, and view the vehicle. Whether the vehicle belongs to a large company or an owner driver, they should be happy to arrange a viewing and may even be able to arrange for the car to seen 'dressed' ready for a wedding, if asked.

Things to check, before making a booking, are:

- will the car be used for weddings other than yours on the day? There could be a knock-on effect of delays earlier in the day, or you may have to sit on someone else's confetti!
- what are the arrangements for a acceptable substitute, should the car break down (preventing it from arriving on time or completing the job) or be sold before the wedding date?
- will the flowers in the car be fresh (unless the usual silk or parchment are preferred)? Bear in mind that fresh flowers may be charged as an extra.
- will ribbons be new (i.e. not used before)?
- will an umbrella be available, in case it rains (golf umbrellas are ideal, since they have a generous spread of protection)?

You should also ask for the vehicle to arrive at least half an hour before it is due to leave the bride's house for the church. (This is a precaution against unexpected delays. Even if the vehicle is 10 to 15 minutes late, the time lost will be absorbed by the half-hour 'cushion' and the ceremony will not be delayed.)

The bridal party

A second car may seem like a luxury, when thinking ahead some six months or so but, on the day itself, it becomes a real boon and, in some cases, an absolute necessity. For a church wedding, the second vehicle will take the bride's mother and the bride's attendants to the church.

If the party is moderately large, say four bridesmaids, the bride's mother and a page boy, an ordinary saloon will not be large enough to transport them all together. The driver may be willing to make two trips from the house to the church or register office but this takes time, 20 to 30 minutes for even the most modest round trip, which may be just too long. Alternatively, a stretched limousine might be the answer. Some extra long vehicles carry seven or eight people in comfort, necessitating only one trip for the whole group.

For a register office ceremony, the bride and her father will need transport and, if the wedding is small, the bride's mother may find herself travelling to the ceremony alone. To provide a second car for her may not be a necessity, but it would almost certainly be welcome. It could be shared with the bride's siblings or the groom's parents and would be most useful after the ceremony, taking family to the reception.

After the ceremony

To the reception

After the ceremony the vehicle that took the bride and her father, or other escort, to the church or register office, will now take the newly-weds to the reception. Sometimes this car will return to the church and pick up the bride's parents, in the absence of a second vehicle being available, but this will delay the reception because the receiving line will not be complete until all four are together with the groom's parents, the best man and the chief bridesmaid or matron-of-honour.

Attendants will also need transport to the reception and, in the absence of a second hired car, family members and guests will need to be pressed into service as unpaid 'taxi' drivers for those who find themselves without wheels at critical moments. However it is arranged, the essentials are that the newly-weds, the bride's parents, the best man/chief bridesmaid or matron-of-honour and groom's parents (if they are to join the receiving line, which is a matter of choice) should arrive at the reception venue as quickly as possible after the ceremony has been completed.

During the reception

During the reception transport will be needed for any number of reasons. Parents with small children need to take them home, Aunt Nell needs to get to the station for the last train and the groom's brother needs to go home to change because little Billy was sick over his suit

– they all may be unable to drive because they are over the limit or there may be a 30 minute wait for a taxi.

A car on call during the reception may not be absolutely necessary, but it can be a blessing as the day and evening pass.

Going away/coming home

Many honeymooners travelling to destinations abroad spend a night or two either at their own home, or at a hotel, after the ceremony and before their flight. Either way, some form of transport is needed to travel to the honeymoon hotel or to the airport/port of embarkation.

Most couples will undertake this journey under their own steam, but the company which supplied the bridal car (providing it was a car, of course, and not a horse-drawn carriage) will arrange for the same vehicle to take the newly-weds to their honeymoon hotel, or to their air or ship departure point, and collect them at the end of their honeymoon. It saves on expensive airport parking and ensures that the atmosphere of the occasion is prolonged for as long as possible.

Prices start at around £180 for a modern limousine, with chauffeur, from a reputable company, to pick up the bride from her home, take her to the church and then take the newly-weds from the church/register office to the reception venue. Vintage cars will cost from around £350 (and often have mileage restriction) and specialist cars, such as an American 1950s Cadillac or a Ford Model T, from £275. A horse-drawn carriage will set you back about £400 upwards.

Horse-drawn vehicles are slower than cars, so journeys which may take a few minutes by car are likely to take much longer in a carriage. Unless the horse(s) are stabled very close to the bride's home, both horse(s) and carriage will be ferried in trailers to a convenient location nearby, such as a car park, where they can be offloaded, tacked-up and dressed. The procedure is reversed when the job is finished and the whole process, including the wedding itself, is likely to take two people five or six hours, plus travelling time from their base, which is why carriages are more costly to hire than cars.

— Photography and video recording —

Finding a photographer is relatively easy, finding a good one, who understands wedding photography, needs a bit more investigation. Good photographers tend to be booked for some time in advance so you should consider booking around five to six months before the wedding, or even a little earlier. Any photographer should be willing, and able, to show you examples of previous commissions, explain how he or she works and what he or she will do on the day, and afterwards. Most work to a tried and tested formula, with a few extras available on request. The photographer should be at the church or register office before the first guests arrive and will take a few shots before the ceremony, generally of the key players, such as the groom and his best man, and the bridesmaids, as they arrive. He or she will photograph the arrival of the bride and her father and, if the minister or registrar permits, as they walk up the aisle. The photographer should also be willing to visit the bride's home before she leaves for the ceremony (to take some pictures in the garden, for example) and to go with the bridal party to a location away from the church for pictures if the church or register office is not photogenic or has insufficient space for pictures. An extra charge may be made for these extra services.

A basic photography package will include around 30 to 40 proof quality pictures, taken before, during (if permitted) and after the ceremony, from which the newly-weds choose roughly half for processing to presentation quality, mounted in a special wedding album. They should be able to keep all the proof-quality pictures as well. For this kind of package, a photographer will charge from around £350.

> One of the most moving moments of the whole day, generally caught by only the quickest of cameras, is the groom's face as he turns to watch his bride walking up the aisle towards him.

Extras may include visiting the church or register office prior to the wedding day to take shots while the building is quiet, and going on to the reception to take pictures of the receiving line, speeches and cutting the cake. There should also be a choice of album, covering a range of cost options. The more experienced the photographer and the more pictures taken, the higher the charges will be. Costs of around £550 to £600, when optional extras are added, are about average but £1,000 or more is by no means unusual, some of which will be paid by guests for their own orders.

The proof photographs are for circulating among friends and relatives so that they may choose examples they wish to keep, which are then ordered from the photographer. Copyright belongs to the photographer and pictures may not be copied without consent. Although, technically, copy pictures can be made from prints, any reputable processing laboratory or photographer, other than the one who took the original pictures, will refuse to do so, since this kind of copying breaks copyright law. If your family is large, or the proofs need to be sent abroad, it is worth asking for two sets of proof prints. The photographer usually keeps negatives for up to two years, but check in order to avoid disappointment later.

Video recording is becoming increasingly popular providing, as it does, a more vibrant record of the day than is possible with photographs alone. As with the photographer, ask to see examples of work before deciding and ask how the recording will actually be made. The best wedding videos come from two (or more) cameras, strategically placed to capture different aspects of the same course of events, edited together afterwards for presentation.

Cameras are generally static, in order to be as unobtrusive as possible to the ceremony and guests. In most cases two cameras is the optimum, since three or more tend to pick each other up, in shot, too often. Editing, and the addition of music and titles, should be included in the price and some companies will add a commentary to the finished product, if asked, as an extra.

The video camera operator will work to a schedule similar to that of the photographer, and they should meet and confer before the day itself to ensure they can work together.

The cost of videoing a wedding varies a great deal around the country and price is not always a good guide to quality. Expect to pay anything from £200 to £1,000, depending on the experience and reputation of the company, location and extras. Some ministers and priests will not permit photography or videoing inside the church; check first to avoid last-minute disappointments.

Flowers

Most florists provide wedding flowers. More than the cake and the reception venue, flowers are a very personal thing for the bride, second only to her choice of dress. With hot houses providing extended flowering seasons almost everywhere, all kinds of flowers are available all year round. Roses at Christmas may be a little more costly, but they are there for the bride who wants them.

Florists will advise on availability, and designs are generally chosen from illustrated catalogues, or the bride may provide a picture of a special design. The most commonly placed order is for a bridal bouquet, sprays for the bridesmaids and buttonholes for the groom, the best man, the bride's father and the ushers. Extras may include pedestal displays for the chancel steps at the church, for the reception venue or for the register office, decorations for the ends of pews and around entrances and exits, an arch under which the newly-weds may have pictures taken, sprays and garlands to decorate the top table at the reception, corsages for the two mothers, headdresses for the bride and her attendants and fresh flowers in the bridal car.

Unlike most of the other services for the wedding, flowers can wait until quite close to the wedding date. Three to four weeks notice is usually sufficient, by which time the florist will know which flowers will be available and at their best for the week of the wedding.

Flowers are usually delivered on the day they are used or, if they are needed very early, late on the day before. Bearing in mind that buttonholes for the men may be part of the order, and the best man may need the ushers' buttonholes quite early, flowers should be delivered/collected in plenty of time.

To keep flowers fresh, spray them liberally with cool, fresh water (preferably distilled, if the local tap water is very hard, since hard water leaves unsightly lime or chalky deposits as it dries) and store them overnight in a cold place or in a refrigerator set at 1 or 2.

If the florist can also see a picture of the dress, she or he will probably make helpful suggestions as to size, design and colour of the bride's flowers, taking into account that the flowers should enhance the whole picture, not overshadow either the dress or the bride.

Most pedestal arrangements are made of two or more pieces fitted together, usually the top bowl, in which flowers are arranged, and the stem of the stand. They are quite heavy, and the flowers themselves are fairly fragile but, with care, they can be transferred from one place to another. This means that flowers used in a church or register office could be moved to the reception while the photographic session is underway, providing there are two or three strong pairs of arms to take care of it. If in doubt, have a word with the florist when placing the orders.

It is occasionally possible to share the expense of these larger displays if there is another wedding on the same day. The minister/priest/ registrar may be willing to put the brides in touch with one another, if asked, to see if it could be arranged.

Fresh flowers are always the favourite, but flowers of silk or parchment are also available and have the advantage of lasting a long time and of being hypoallergenic. They are, of course, more costly than the real thing.

> Symbolising spring, and new life, flowers are a plea for fertility and healthy children. Often strong-smelling herbs were entwined with flowers, or even used by themselves, since it was thought that the strong smells would help to ward off bad luck, evil spirits and ill health.

Since there are so many ways of using flowers, and the time of year makes such a difference to cost, it is impossible to say what the total average expenditure is likely to be but, using seasonal flowers, a bridal bouquet is likely to cost around £25 to £35, a bridesmaid's spray about £10 to £15, buttonholes around £2 each and, as a rough guide, a 1.5 m (5 ft) pedestal display anything from £50 upwards.

There are specialist companies which will arrange for the bridal bouquet to be dried, pressed and mounted, as a permanent reminder and keepsake of the day. Prices vary, according to the size of the bouquet, the type of flowers used and the size of frame, but a good rule of thumb would be to allow between £40 to £80.

Cake

Using a local bakery, or the chef at the reception venue (if there is one) is the most convenient way to arranging for a wedding cake to be made. Shape and size will dictate how many people the cake will provide for and the baker will help with estimating what weight of cake will be needed.

The modern wedding cake was introduced into England from France in the seventeenth century, probably by Royalists returning from exile when King Charles II was restored to his throne. One superstition holds that if the bride-to-be whispers to a beehive that she is to marry, the bees make especially sweet and powerful honey for the honeymoon drink, mead. In return she makes an offering to the hive of something sweet, such as the wedding cake with its sugar coating, from the wedding breakfast table.

Generally the cake is chosen from a catalogue of photographs, and most bakers will mix and match decorations to individual requirements

Wedding cakes are generally rich fruit cakes but these are not to everyone's taste. One tier, made out of sponge cake, iced and decorated to match the fruit layers gives guests a choice.

Rich fruit cakes will last a long time, if stored properly, and will often taste better if allowed to mature. However, if the baker makes cakes well in advance and then stores them inadequately, they will be dry and lacking in flavour so ask to try a piece of one of his or her cakes before placing your order. A reputable baker should be happy to provide samples.

The baker, or the reception venue manager, should be able to supply a cake stand and slice for the wedding day. There may be an extra charge, but it is unlikely to be very much. The cost of the cake itself will depend on its size and the complexity of its decorations: a small two-tier cake should be around £130.

Stationery

Every good stationer and printer will have catalogues of wedding stationery. The range is huge, from the simplest card to the most comprehensive collection, from chocolate-box-pretty to supremely elegant.

Designs are pre-printed and there are generally several typefaces to choose from as well. Details of the wedding are sent to the printer with an order, which will take four to eight weeks to deliver, depending on the time of the year. Matched collections include:

- invitations to the church/register office only
- invitations to the ceremony and reception
- invitations to the reception only
- reply cards
- orders of service
- table name cards
- cake boxes
- table napkins
- book matches
- thank you cards.

There is generally a minimum order and prices start from around £30 for £40 simple cards.

Personalised stationery is becoming more common and certainly adds something to the image and ambiance of the occasion. If your *Yellow Pages*, under 'Wedding Services', does not have a listing for a stationery designer, ask a local printer and/or check the classified advertisements in your local paper. Bridal magazines are also a good source of information.

Commissioning a designer to create your wedding stationery is one way of putting a personal mark on a wedding. Designer stationery may take a little longer to deliver than pre-printed items, so taking into account that invitations should be sent out no later than six weeks before the wedding, and preferably eight to nine weeks before, a first consultation with the designer should really take place around four or five months before the wedding.

One bride, who wanted unique and personal stationery, commissioned a graphic designer to produce cards with a traditional Chinese dragon on the front and, on the inside, the Chinese horoscopes of her groom and herself, highlighting their compatibility.

Prices will be higher than for mass-produced stationery, but by how much will depend on the amount of work involved, the quality of the paper used and the number of items ordered. It is important to fix a deadline for completion and the price right at the beginning in order to avoid unpleasant surprises.

How many to order

You should allow sufficient numbers of invitations to the ceremony and reception, plus reply cards if they are being provided as a convenience to guests, so that one of each can be sent to:

- every family being invited (that is couples and their children under the age of 18 years)
- every married or engaged couple
- every individual (every person aged over 18 years of age, whether living alone, at their family home with parents or with a partner)

In addition keep spares for those last minute additions or those lost in the mail.

The term 'and friend' may be added to an invitation to individuals and they should include the name of the friend they intend to bring with them in the reply accepting the invitation.

If guests are to be invited only to the reception and not the ceremony, or to the ceremony but not to the reception, separate invitations and reply cards will be needed.

When ordering preprinted stationery, discounts to prices are sometimes available for volume so it can be advantageous to make all the decisions, such as the form of the church service and the music that will be played for the order of service, and so on, and order a complete set of stationery all at once.

If the reception is to be held at a hotel, the function co-ordinator will probably offer place cards and napkins as part of the package. If the bride wishes to keep an overall theme by following through her own choice of stationery, the hotel may be willing to undertake the calligraphy work of making up the place cards, using the bride's own stationery, but are unlikely to offer a price reduction if both stationery and calligraphy are done elsewhere.

Fees

Church wedding fees tend to vary around the country, but register office fees are fixed, and are the same everywhere.

Register Office	–	£18 on the day of giving notice to the registrar
		£21.50 on the wedding day itself

Flowers and music are not provided, but may be brought in by the couple being married, or their families, by arrangement with the registrar.

Church of England	–	£90, varies but includes the caretaker (to prepare the church and close up after the ceremony) and generally the organist as well: choir and bells are extra
Catholic Church	–	£25 to £50, varies around the country
Methodist Church	–	£20 to £40, varies around the country
Baptist Church	–	£30 to £50 varies around the country

For Catholic, Methodist and Baptist churches, the caretaker and organist fees may not be included. One copy of the entry of the marriage in the Marriage Registration Book (the marriage certificate) is provided, without extra charge, but a choir and bells will be charged as extras, according to local rates.

Insurance

This is an absolute must and any broker will be able to find a company to provide a suitable policy and advise you when to take it out. Only one or two insurance companies handle wedding insurance, so shopping around probably will not help reduce costs, but premiums are fairly modest so this should not be a problem. Expect premiums to be around £50 for basic cover, with extras available to suit different circumstances.

A recommended minimum level of cover should include:

- loss, theft, damage to/of any item of clothing (bridal gown, brides-maids' dresses, accessories and menswear, whether bought or hired)
- loss, damage or failure of photographs, howsoever caused
- illness or death of bride or groom or parent of either
- failure of any contracted supplier to provide the goods or services agreed upon at the time of agreed delivery
- loss, theft or damage to/of wedding presents
- loss, theft or damage to/of wedding rings.

No insurance company will insure against anyone changing their mind, whether it is an attendant, one or both of the bridal couple, or a parent of either of them.

Cover is usually restricted to the cost of replacement, but it is worth asking if additional cover, such as compensation for stress, or for extra expenses incurred as a result of any loss or damage, might also be included in a policy.

An insurance policy proved invaluable when the bride's father had a heart attack the day before the wedding. The wedding was postponed since the family's concern through-out that night and the next few days was concentrated on him. Fortunately he recovered well and the wedding went ahead at a later date. The insurance policy covered the costs of cancelling the catered reception and flowers, reprinting the stationery, and lost deposits on transport, photography, video recording, menswear hire and entertainment. Dresses, accessories and the cake were all used at the rescheduled wedding, three months later.

Wedding arrangers

If you have only limited time to devote to arranging your wedding, prefer to have your wedding arranged by professionals, are unsure whether you can do the job well enough, or feel that other people's well-meaning advice (or dare we say, interference) is more than you can cope with, then employing an arranger might be the answer.

Most companies which advertise this service are actually information bureaux, acting as agents and sending out information on all kinds of wedding services under their own corporate banner. It is then up to the client to make contact directly with suppliers and conclude arrangements. Generally this is offered as a free service and, in a way, it is since the enquirer/client is not charged directly for the information provided. However, companies promoted by agents in this way pay a commission, or introduction fee, a cost which they must recover somehow. It almost invariably turns up in the client's bill, hidden in the overall charges.

Companies that offer a genuine arrangement service, that is those that choreograph the whole wedding from beginning to end, are few and far between in the United Kingdom at present, although they are common in other countries, particularly the United States. These companies may have a financial arrangement with the suppliers of wedding services they use in arranging a client's wedding, or they may charge the client a fee, based on the size and shape of the wedding.

In this latter system, the arrangers are free to use any supplier they, or the client, wishes since their own financial advantage is not a factor. As well as giving more choice, this may also mean lower costs since the businesses used have a vested interest (the possibility of repeat business from the arranger) to encourage them to deliver quality and value.

Gifts

Gift list

Few brides are entirely comfortable with the principle of a wedding gift list but it is a boon to guests, allowing them to choose something they know the couple wants within a price range they can afford.

If the newly-weds are setting up a completely new home, the list will almost certainly be a long one, containing expensive items as well as the relatively inexpensive. If their home is already established they may need very little or they may list items to replace those which are old and/or worn. Whatever the situation, the wedding gift list should be as comprehensive as possible so that guests have plenty of choice. Even expensive items should be included since it gives the opportunity for people to club together for a gift really worth giving, if they wish. A sample gift list is included in the Appendix (*see* p161).

There are several ways of handling a gift list to ensure it receives a wide circulation. The bride may choose a shop with branches nation-wide and visit the manager of her local store to find out whether they are able to handle her list. She then sends a copy of the list to every guest. The guest visits their own local branch of the store and, work-ing with the manager or designated deputy, chooses a gift, the details of which are telephoned or faxed through to the branch nearest to the bride's home. Checking that that particular item has not been chosen already by someone else, the gift is selected, wrapped and delivered to the bride's home, with a suitable card. If the gift has been chosen by someone else, a message goes back to the guest asking them to choose again. Some stores will perform this service without charge, because of the benefits of business it brings them, but some will charge a fee.

Another way is to split the list into three or four equal parts and send each part, with the names of one third or one quarter of the guests, to one guest whose name should appear at the top of the guest list. This person chooses the gift they will send, crosses off their own name from the list along with the item they have chosen to give, and sends the list on to the person named next.

Probably the simplest alternative is for the bride or her mother to manage the list themselves. A copy of the list goes out to every invited guest who then calls the bride or her mother to discuss their choice and check that someone else has not already made the same choice.

Good manners suggest that, whichever method of managing the list is chosen, it should not be released until after invitations have been sent out. Too soon and the invitation takes on a rather mercenary complexion and too late may create difficulties in managing it suc-cessfully. A week or two later would be ideal. Everyone needs to know how the list is being managed and guidance should be included with each copy sent out.

Parents' gifts

Not quite a tradition yet, it is common for the couple to give presents to their parents. The gifts should commemorate the day, reflecting the couple's love and thanks for the years of care their parents have given them. Suggestions include engraved crystal, ornamental photograph frames (perhaps silver) or the bridal bouquet, dried and mounted in a picture frame, or a piece of porcelain.

Attendants' gifts

The bride and groom normally give a small gift to each of their attendants in order to thank them for what they have done. As far as possible, the gift should have some connection with the wedding and be personal to the recipient.

For a church wedding, the gifts may be, for example, a prayer book with an inscription from the bride and groom, a piece of jewellery, such as a pendant cross or crucifix or an illuminated scroll commemorating the day. The bridal couple usually present the gifts before the wedding so they may be used (the prayer book) or worn (jewellery) on the day.

Honeymoon

A honeymoon is an opportunity to wind down from the nervous tension and excitement of preparation and the wedding day and, with so many travel companies offering packaged holidays at moderate prices, it needn't cost the earth.

Traditionally the honeymoon is taken immediately after the wedding and arranging it is the groom's responsibility. If the honeymoon is to be spent in the United Kingdom the couple may wish to travel on the day of the wedding, leaving the reception to do so, driving off into the sunset with confetti blowing everywhere and tin cans tied to the rear bumper of the car.

Most honeymoons nowadays are of two or three weeks duration, not the original 'moon', or lunar month, of earlier tradition. Even so, a change of pace and place after the adrenaline rush of the countdown to a wedding day, is generally most welcome. A honeymoon can be romantic almost anywhere, whether it is spent ten miles from home or halfway around the world.

Going abroad is a little less convenient, since the majority of holiday flights leave at inconvenient times of the day and, often, midweek. In this case, the favoured option is to spend the wedding night in the hotel which hosted the reception, or one very close by, and travel the next day. Some newly-weds postpone the honeymoon until a more convenient time, or may opt not to take one at all. It's not unusual for children to go on honeymoon with their newly-wed parents and some couples even take parents or other relatives with them.

Arranging a honeymoon is no different from arranging any other sort of trip in that reservations must be made, visas applied for (where appropriate), passports obtained (if needed and/or not already held) and health checks/precautions carried out. If the wedding is to be held during a busy holiday season, such as the period between mid-July and the end of August, or over Christmas or Easter, then reservations are best made early, say around seven to eight months before the wedding, especially if the destination is popular.

The honeymoon is so called because mead, a strongly alcoholic drink made of fermented honey, was served to newlyweds during the first month (or moon) of their married life. It was said to promote fertility and early conception. A modern cynic may say this had as much to do with the loosening of inhibitions brought about by copious amounts of alcohol than by any magical properties of the brew!

If the bride already holds her own passport it will not be necessary to change it to show her married name. She may continue to use it until it expires, but should keep her marriage certificate with it while travelling in order to avoid any possible confusion.

While planning for health needs on the honeymoon, such as vaccinations, the couple may wish to seek a little extra advice from a GP or family planning clinic. Unless they wish to begin a family fairly quickly after their marriage, or already have a satisfactory routine, this is the time to discuss available family planning options and decide what to do. The bride will also probably have a good idea, by this time, whether her menstrual cycle is likely to interrupt her full enjoyment of the wedding or honeymoon and, if alerted early enough, her GP may be able to help here, too.

4

BUDGETING
AND BOOKING

Setting the budget

By now you will have a good idea what sort of wedding you want and should have a working budget to begin with. You will alter and refine your plans continually over the next few months, so be prepared to be flexible while still keeping your objectives clear in your mind.

Planning a wedding is not difficult, but you will need some organisational skill and a lot of patience. In this chapter we look at the main aspects of the wedding, and identify the people you should see, and talk to, and how to keep it all under control.

Without a doubt, a wedding is quite possibly the single most expensive event that a family or individual is likely to arrange. The preparation of any budget calls for information and a wedding budget is no different, it is a matter of knowing what is needed, (keeping a little flexibility in reserve just in case your first choice is already booked, is too expensive or is simply not available) and researching the options carefully. Remember, the client writes the cheques, if a supplier is not satisfactory in some way, look for another.

Ask friends for recommendations, use the *Yellow Pages* and local newspapers, call in at local shops. Some providers will send photographs (of cars, for example), some will ask if they can meet you to discuss your needs and some will suggest a visit to their shops or offices. Explain the requirement fully and ask for estimates – check that like is being comparing with like and bear in mind that price may not always be a good guide to quality.

With a mental picture of the wedding in mind, or better still, a written plan, it is quite easy to add figures against the key elements. The resulting budget will provide a very rough figure of the sort of costs to be expected. The emphasis here is on 'rough' because suppliers will be unable to guarantee estimates until firm commitments are made, with dates, times, numbers and so on, and a deposit is paid. As a rough guide, a traditional church wedding for between 100 to 120 guests will cost approximately £8,000 to £12,000, excluding honeymoon. It can be achieved for less (should your budget be tight); you could also spend more (if money is no object) and we will show you how to do both in later chapters. Register office weddings tend to be less formal and more relaxed, and so tend to cost less. An average cost for 60 guests would be around £3,500 to £4,500.

Here we look at two possible budgets to see where the major costs are incurred.

Example 1

A Church of England wedding, with 120 guests, is planned for late morning, with a reception to be held at a local golf club. There will be four bridesmaids, (two adults and two children), and four ushers. The bridesmaids will meet at the bride's home where a beauty therapist and a hairdresser will do the bride's make-up and hair.

The bride and her father will travel to the church in an Edwardian landau, pulled by two horses and attended by two footmen in appropriate period outfits. It will wait at the church to take the newly-weds to the reception after the ceremony. A limousine will be hired to take the bridesmaids and the bride's mother to the church, and then make two trips to the reception, with the bride's parents and then with the bridesmaids. The bridal car is to return later, first to take the couple to a hotel for their wedding night, and then to take the bride's parents and the chief bridesmaid home, with the wedding presents and remainder of the cake. The limousine will collect the bridal couple the next morning and take them to the airport for their honeymoon flight, meeting them on their return two weeks later.

The bride will carry a large bouquet of roses and evergreens, with a fresh-flower headdress to match. Each bridesmaid has a small, hand-held posy. The florist provides two pedestal arrangements for the church, which are moved to stand at either end of the reception top table as the photographer does his work at the church, and 24 posies for pew ends. The groom, best man, the bride's father and ushers will all wear buttonhole flowers.

Guests will be welcomed to the reception with a glass of buck's fizz and then sit down to a silver service three-course meal, plus coffee and mints. Wine will be served with the meal and pieces of a three-tier wedding cake will be served during the speeches, with a glass of champagne for the toasts. The club bar, where guests buy their own drinks, opens when the tables have been cleared. In the late afternoon 30 of the guests leave, but 40 more arrive to join an evening celebration, with a live band and a disco, that continues until around 11 p.m.

Budget

Bridal gown and accessories	£1,400.00
Bridesmaids' outfits (purchased)	£320.00
Beauty therapist/hairdresser (bride only)	£50.00
Menswear (groom, best man, bride's father and ushers), hired	£420.00
Flowers	£380.00
Photographer	£525.00
Transport, horse-drawn carriage	£450.00
limousine	£240.00
Stationery and postage	£540.00
Rings	£235.00
Cake	£220.00
Reception/accommodation	£6,500.00
Entertainment	£500.00
Going-away outfits (bride and groom)	£550.00
Fees, including organist, bells and caretaker	£140.00
Insurance	£175.00
Honeymoon, Italy x2 weeks	£2,500.00
Total	£15,145.00

Example 2

A register office wedding at mid-morning, with 60 guests, is to be followed by a short reception at a local hotel. A hired limousine take the bride and her sister to the register office and, after the ceremony, takes the newly-weds to the reception. The groom will be accompanied by a friend, who will stand as one of the witnesses and the bride will enter the register office with her sister, who will stand as the other. The bride and her sister both carry posies of seasonal flowers. The bridal couple have provided a music tape to be played during the ceremony.

The reception will be held at a local hotel where guests will be welcomed with a glass of sherry. Taped music will play in the background and a finger buffet, with wine, is provided. The bar is open for those who wish to purchase other types of drinks. Speeches are made and the cake is cut and a glass of champagne is provided for everyone for the toasts.

The newly-weds leave at 3 p.m. for their honeymoon at an English country cottage in the New Forest.

Budget

Bridal gown and accessories	£500.00
Sister's outfit	£150.00
Menswear (2), purchased	£400.00
Reception	£1,800.00
Transport	£280.00
Rings	£180.00
Cake	£140.00
Photographer	£320.00
Stationery and postage	£200.00
Fees	£40.00
Flowers	£50.00
Insurance	£40.00
Honeymoon	£600.00
Total	£4,700.00

In the two examples above a register office wedding is seen to be less expensive than a church wedding; this reflects trends as they actually are although it is, of course, possible to spend less than £10,000 on a church wedding and much more than £4,000 on a register office ceremony.

These examples use nationwide averages and cover a wide range of regional variation as well as personal circumstances.

—————— Who pays for what? ——————

Traditionally, a wedding is hosted by the bride's parents, who arrange and pay for almost, but not quite, everything. However, the days of rigid etiquette are long gone and any arrangement that suits your circumstances is fine. Remember, though, the old maxim of too many cooks – the more people that there are involved, the more important it will be to be well organised yourself, in order to make sure everything is done on time.

Weddings can be extremely expensive events, and few families are in the fortunate position of not needing to budget carefully. Nevertheless, even in a traditional situation, expenditure is often spread over quite a lengthy period of time and can generally be planned in advance with a fair degree of accuracy.

Traditional responsibilities

The bride

- bridesmaid's dresses and accessories (unless the bridesmaids are to keep them afterwards, in which case they pay for their own)
- own dress and accessories
- hair/make-up on the day
- wedding gift for the groom
- share of gifts to attendants and parents
- groom's wedding ring
- going-away outfit

If the bride has no income or financial resources of her own, her father or father-substitute will pay for these.

DOWRIES

The dowry may be money, goods or livestock or a mixture of all three. The bride's family send the dowry with her to her new home as a gift for her husband. It may represent different things, such as the value the family place on her or as a coded message telling the husband that he is expected to keep her in style which the value of the dowry represents. In European history the husband was supposed to return the dowry if his bride proved to be an unsatisfactory wife and he felt obliged to send her home. In reality, many such wives were kept as virtual prisoners by husbands who would not, or could not, repay the dowry. A father of daughters could easily bankrupt himself providing dowries for them all or, alternatively, he might have forbidden them to marry or simply neglected to find them husbands.

In Greece the custom has evolved into a charming tradition which takes place during the dancing that follows the wedding ceremony. As the couple dance, their guests pin paper money to their clothes as they swirl past. Everyone is expected to be generous and there is, of course, every reason to invite as many people as possible.

The bride's father

- press announcements
- the reception (venue, food, entertainment, welcome drinks for guests, wine with the meal and champagne for toasts), and decorations
- transport for himself and the bride, plus the attendants and the bride's mother and groom's parents, if appropriate, to the church/register office and then to the reception
- flowers for the bride and her attendants, plus church and reception decorations
- stationery and postage
- his own, and the bride's mother's, outfits for the day
- a wedding present for his daughter and her new husband
- photographer and video maker
- insurance
- overnight accommodation for close family, unless they offer to pay for their own

The groom

BRIDE PRICE

The custom of putting a price on the bride dictates that the prospective groom approach the father of his intended bride for permission to marry and is told the value her family places on her as a housekeeper, companion to her mother, dutiful daughter and so on. The hopeful groom would then accumulate this wealth, again either in goods, money or livestock, according to custom, and present it to the bride's father in return for his permission to marry. A father of beautiful and accomplished daughters could become wealthy this way. It was not unknown, nor is it still, for the bride to persuade her father to set her price too high for the poor hopeful groom, if she has no wish to hear his proposal, or indeed for a father to use the same ruse to hold on to a daughter he has no intention of losing!

- his own outfit for the day
- buttonholes for himself and his attendants
- the bride's wedding ring
- a wedding gift for the bride
- a share of gifts to attendants, with the bride
- transport for himself and his new wife away from the reception to their wedding night destination
- the honeymoon
- church/register office fees, including extras such as the choir and bell ringer (on the day of the wedding, the best man takes care of any outstanding fees with funds provided by the groom)

For the superstitious, the amount of money the groom gives to the best man to pay fees should be slightly in excess of what is required and should not be the exact amount, requiring change to be given. This is to ensure that the fees have been paid in full and the best man has not made a profit on the deal! Historically, if the full amount of fees was not paid to the minister, and a promise to pay was not fulfilled within a specified time, the minister could declare the marriage invalid.

The best man

- his own outfit for the day
- a wedding present for the newly-weds
- transport to take the groom and himself away from the church/ register office to the reception

Ushers

- their own outfits for the day

When to pay

You will almost always be asked for a deposit when you agree to buy goods or services. The trader will ask you to sign an agreement, or contract, which will also serve as a receipt for your deposit. The price you agree now should be the price you actually pay. Most weddings are planned around nine to twelve months in advance and any intended price rises should be already included in the price you are quoted. check that this is the case before you pay a deposit. Above all, make sure you read the contract carefully; once you have signed it and the deposit is paid there will be a penalty should you change your mind, most commonly this is the loss of your deposit.

The deposit may be anything between a token flat rate up to 20 to 30 per cent of the full price or estimated final cost. It is also quite common to be asked to pay the balance before the wedding day, a month before is the most usual. Deposits will generally be non-refundable although some traders will return a deposit if the cancellation allows sufficient time for another booking to be taken.

Some will ask for stage payments, for example, the caterer may ask for a booking deposit, another payment a month or so before the wedding and a final payment when final numbers are known and this, too, is fairly common. Check each trader's policy before booking.

Staged payments may be spread out over several months, making the cost of expensive parts of the wedding a little easier to meet, but there are risks attached. A reliable trader should deposit your advance payments in a special client-account and keep a check on how much you have paid and how much/when expenditure has been incurred on your behalf. If this facility is not available, you would be wise to re-consider a trader's request for advance or staged payments.

Loans

It is possible to borrow money from banks and finance houses to pay for a wedding, in the same way that money for a new car or furniture can be borrowed. Most commonly this is done through a personal loan secured by an approved asset, such as property or a life assurance policy. Interest rates vary according to the prevailing financial climate but, once arranged, are fixed for the term of repayments which may be anything but are usually one to five years.

It is wise to get approval in principle for a loan well in advance, then arrange to draw on the facility only when expenditure is at its highest, otherwise you could find yourself paying interest on borrowed money that sits in a bank account for weeks, or months, before it is really needed.

Insurance

One expense that may seem to be low priority but is, in fact, very important, is the insurance cover. It will not cover against either the bride or groom changing their mind but it should cover accidents, losses and thefts to clothes, people and facilities, or failure of suppliers to deliver contracted services, which may prevent the wedding going ahead or being completed satisfactorily.

Liability will be limited to specific maximum values and cover will come into force only at a predetermined date of so many weeks before the wedding date.

5

WHO DOES WHAT?

Traditional roles are still the most common when it comes to arranging a church wedding, although more and more grooms now take an active part in making arrangements and sharing the financial responsibility.

Church weddings generally involve more roles than civil ceremonies, although now that more alternatives to the local register office are available, it seems likely that some civil ceremonies will be more elaborate in the future.

Whichever type of wedding you choose, the first step is to make contact with the minister or priest, the function co-ordinator at the venue you have chosen for a civil ceremony, or the local registrar. At this stage, which will probably be 9–12 months before the wedding, you will simply be reserving a date, but this is just the beginning.

Bride and groom

The bride and groom do much of the preliminary information gathering and planning together but are soon joined by others, such as the bride's parents and the senior attendants, who all have roles to play. If the ceremony is to be held at a register office, and especially if this is a second marriage for either the bride or groom, or both, it is likely that the bridal couple will arrange everything themselves.

Before the wedding

- Visit the minister, priest, function co-ordinator and/or registrar, as appropriate, to discuss arrangements regarding music, flowers, costs and so on;
- Obtain copies of relevant documents, if necessary;
- Attend marriage preparation classes, or instruction as suggested by the minister or priest;
- Choose attendants and invite them to participate;
- Choose and purchase wedding rings;
- Attend rehearsals.

The wedding day

- Under the guidance of the minister/priest or registrar, complete the wedding ceremony;
- Co-operate with the photographer and video recorder (as appropriate) to produce a record of events;
- With both sets of parents, the best man and senior bridesmaid, welcome guests to the reception;
- Cut the cake either before the meal is served, or after the speeches, whichever has been decided.

After the wedding

If the honeymoon is not to be taken immediately:

- Return any hired clothing to the hire shop;
- Send off the bouquets to be dried, pressed and mounted, as appropriate;
- Send thankyou letters for all gifts not yet acknowledged;
- With the bride's mother, send out pieces of cake to all invited guests who were unable to attend;
- Thank suppliers for good service received, as appropriate.

Bride

The bride's responsibilities are almost always shared with another, either the groom, or her mother or her senior attendant, unless the wedding is to be very low key and simple. If she is to take care of everything herself, she will not, at least, need to be concerned with co-ordinating the efforts of several different people, with all the hazards inherent in that situation!

A list of what she needs to do can be compiled from looking at the responsibilities normally fulfilled by the mother of the bride and by the senior female attendant, taking only those items which are relevant, of course.

Groom

In a traditionally arranged wedding, the groom has few direct responsibilities of his own except to choose his best man and ushers, arrange transport for himself and his bride to leave the reception and arrange and pay for the honeymoon. If the wedding is very simple, with no parental involvement he will almost certainly share arrangements and financial responsibility with his bride, as already described.

Chief bridesmaid/matron-of-honour

The chief bridesmaid, or matron-of-honour, is the bride's right hand from the day she accepts the commission weeks, or even months, before the wedding until her duties are fulfilled, which could be as late as the day the newly-weds come back from their honeymoon.

Before the wedding

In the period immediately prior to the wedding the chief bridesmaid or matron-of-honour will:

- Arrange, and pay for, her own outfit, in consultation with the bride and bride's mother on styles and colours. (The bride may pay if the style of the outfit is such that it is not suitable for wearing on other, subsequent, occasions.);
- Help the bride to choose other attendants' outfits;
- Help with wedding arrangements as much as possible;
- Arrange a 'hen' night for the bride (*see* p77);
- Attend the wedding rehearsal;
- Ensure that flowers for the bridesmaids are ordered and delivered to the right place at the right time;
- Arrive to help the bride and her mother prepare around two to three hours before the ceremony.

The wedding day

On the day of the wedding the chief bridesmaid or matron-of-honour will:

- Make sure that the bride has a change of clothes, and somewhere convenient to change, after the reception, if necessary (liaise with the bride's mother who may have taken care of this);
- Make sure that tissues, lipstick, comb, mirror, etc. are easily available to the bride throughout the wedding day;
- Make sure all the bride's attendants arrive at the church with plenty of time to spare;
- Take the bride's flowers, and anything else she is carrying, to free her hands when she arrives at the chancel steps;
- With the best man, and the bridegroom's parents, accompany the bride and groom to the vestry to witness the singing of the Register;
- After the signing, return the bride's gloves, flowers, etc. and join the procession on the left-hand side of the best man, directly behind the bride and groom, to leave the church;
- After the newly-weds have driven away from the church, travel with the best man and other attendants to the reception and join the receiving line to welcome guests;
- Record every gift received on the wedding day, and who gave them. Wedding presents should be unwrapped and display for everyone to see;
- Make sure the bridal bouquet is stored somewhere safe and cool during the reception and retrieved and given back to the bride as the newly-weds leave;
- Help the bride out of her wedding dress when she wishes to change, take care of the dress and make sure it is returned either to the hire company the next day, if appropriate, or to the bride's home or other place agreed upon.

After the wedding

While the newly-weds are on their honeymoon, the chief bridesmaid or matron-of-honour should:

- Take the bridal bouquet to be dried and pressed, if appropriate, the next day;
- Arrange to be at the newly-weds home when they return from their

honeymoon, if at all possible, making sure that the house is warm and that there are groceries, such as coffee/tea, bread, milk, and so on, in the kitchen;

- Write to the bride and groom to thank them for their gift (*see* p77);
- Write to the bride's parents to thank them for their hospitality.

Bridesmaids

Part of a bridesmaid's role is to be polite and patient all through the day, quite a tall order when even the most smoothly run wedding can sometimes seem like a city centre in the rush hour!

> The title 'bridesmaid' has two separate, and literal, meanings. Traditionally bridesmaids should be maids, in the sense that they should be young, single girls. They should also be able to fulfil the role of lady's maid for the bride.

Before the wedding

The bridesmaids' responsibilities before the wedding day are:

- Attend rehearsals of the wedding ceremony;
- Help the bride choose outfits (paying for their own if they are to keep them afterwards);
- Help with child attendants, choosing outfits and making sure that children attend fittings, and so on.

The wedding day

On the day of the wedding the bridesmaids should:

- Arrive at the bride's home (or wherever she is preparing for the wedding day) two to three hours before the ceremony is due to take place, and be on hand to run errands, take messages, protect the bride from stress and aggravation as much as possible, and help her with her clothes, hair and make-up;
- Carry any small items of personal grooming that the bride may need during the day, as requested by the chief bridesmaid or matron-of-honour;

- At the church (having arrived with the bride's mother), wait outside for the bride and her father to arrive, then help the bride to straighten her gown, headdress and so on, and make sure her shoes are clean (especially if it is a wet day) before the walk up the aisle;
- Take care of junior attendants in the church and throughout the photographic session and reception;
- Progress up the aisle behind the bride and her father;
- With one of the ushers, walking on his left-hand side, process down the aisle after the ceremony behind the best man and the chief bridesmaid or matron-of-honour;
- Circulate among guests at the reception, offering drinks and refreshments;
- Distribute pieces of the wedding cake (unless the reception arrangements include waiting staff, in which case they will take care of this);
- Generally assist the bride and chief bridesmaid or matron-of-honour, as requested.

Child attendants may be too young to be of much practical help, but they will almost certainly appreciate being involved as much as possible, no matter how small the task.

> One four-year-old bridesmaid stood still and silent whenever she was asked to do so, which was several times during the ceremony and photographic session, much to the amazement of her otherwise harassed mother. When asked why she was behaving like a miniature angel, she said that she had been asked to take care of the bride's handkerchief and was determined not to drop or crease it because it was very important.

After the bride has reached the chancel steps and handed her flowers to the chief bridesmaid or matron-of-honour, the bridesmaids and other attendants may sit down in the front pew on their left, with the bride's mother, leaving room for the bride's father to join them as soon as his duties have been concluded, or stand on the bride's left-hand side, about one pace behind her.

Minister

Chancel steps

Bride   Groom

Bridesmaids   Bride's father   Best man   Ring bearer

After the register has been signed, and the bride and groom process down the aisle to leave the church, the bridesmaids fall into step behind the newly-weds, each adult bridesmaid on the left arm of an usher.

During the photographic shoot outside the church, bridesmaids help the photographer to ensure that the bride's gown and veil are arranged to the best advantage. Throughout the day they should make themselves useful to the bride and her mother, in much the same way that they did while getting ready.

After the wedding

The bridesmaids, or their parents if they are young children, should:

- Write to the bride and groom, after the wedding, to thank them for their gifts;
- Write to the bride's parents to thank them for their hospitality;
- Arrange for their dresses to be cleaned and return them to the newly-weds' home, as soon as is practicable, if they are not to keep them.

Flower girl

Usually quite a young girl, around the ages of six to eight years, she may be dressed in the same style and colours as the bridesmaids or in a different, but complementary outfit, according to the bride's taste. She walks in front of the bride and her father as they progress up the aisle, scattering flower petals as she goes. Staying with the bridesmaids throughout the ceremony, she then walks ahead of them in the procession leaving the church, directly in front of the bride and groom.

The role and tradition of the flower girl comes from times when sanitation was poor and street smells, which were also thought to be connected with the causes of disease, could be extremely pungent! Many people carried oranges studded with cloves, others carried little pouches containing dried herbs or flowers, all to mask the more unpleasant smells in the streets.

After the wedding the flower girls should write to the bride and groom, thanking them for their gift (*see* p77) and to the bride's parents, to thank them for their hospitality. If she is very young her parents should write on her behalf.

Page and ring bearer

Page

The page is usually a small boy of around six to eight years of age, often dressed in satin knee breeches or a miniature tartan kilt, whose duty is to carry the bridal gown train clear of the ground. He should be ready as the bridal car pulls up outside the church to collect the trailing edge of the train in both hands and carry it as the bride enters the church and moves up the aisle. When she and her father arrive at the chancel steps the page arranges the train on the floor behind the bride then slips into his seat next to the bridesmaids and the bride's mother in the front pew, left-hand side.

As the procession leaves the church, he carries the train until the bride and guests gather for photographs outside.

Ring bearer

Often the ring bearer is another small boy, although there is no reason why a little girl should not fill the role. The ring bearer normally will be dressed in either a miniature lounge or morning suit, or in satin knee breeches, according to the bride's taste. The ring bearer, like ushers, is really the best man's man, displaying the ring for all to see before it is slipped on the bride's finger.

The tradition of the ring bearer has its origins in more lawless times when street crime was rife and pockets were slit, often unnoticed by their owners, in order to 'liberate' their contents. By entrusting the ring to someone else, often a young servant, for safe keeping the best man could concentrate on looking after the groom.

The ring bearer should go to the church with the groom and best man, waiting with them until the bride arrives. One of the ushers should tell the best man as soon as the bride's transport pulls up outside, and that is the signal for the ring bearer to go to the entrance to join the bridesmaids.

The ring bearer shows the bride the ring, before she enters the church, so that she will be assured that her groom is already there and has every intention of marrying her today.

The ring(s) is/are pinned to a small, decorated pillow, or carried in a velvet-lined basket, by the ring bearer, who follows directly behind the bride and her father, and in front of the bridesmaids, up the aisle. When they arrive at the chancel steps, the ring bearer moves to the right, standing on the right of the best man, facing the choir and altar. The best man should take the ring, and hold it himself, as the minister begins the service. The ring bearer then sits down in the front pew, right-hand side, where he will be joined by the best man as soon as his duties are finished.

After the wedding, the page and the ring bearer should write to the bride and groom, thanking them for their gift (*see* p77) and to the bride's parents for their hospitality. If they are very young their parents should write on their behalf.

Best man

The best man, or groomsman, is a key player in preparing for a wedding, and on the day itself. Usually a friend of the groom of some years standing, perhaps from school, university or first job, the best man should be someone who knows the groom quite well because he will be asked for advice and practical help during the planning stage of the wedding and will be expected to give a witty and amusing speech at the reception, arguably the most daunting task that any young man will undertake in the name of friendship!

> Traditionally, the best man was the groom's companion and protector through the period prior to the wedding, making sure that nothing prevented the groom from attending his wedding in perfect mental, physical and financial health.

The best man's first task is to meet the bride and her family, if they don't already know each other, and the groom should arrange this introduction as soon as possible. From then on his responsibilities are many and varied.

Before the wedding

In the period prior to the wedding day the best man should:

- Be party to discussions and decisions in planning the wedding, as much as is possible and feasible;
- Help the groom to choose the ushers and explain their duties to them, making sure they understand and attend the rehearsal;
- With the groom, decide on what they, and the ushers will wear to the wedding and make sure arrangements for purchase or hire are made in good time;
- Prepare and practise a speech for the reception (this should be of five to six minutes' duration: witty and amusing is fine, stories that embarrass are not);
- When the guest list has been drawn up, discuss with the groom any special arrangements that may be needed (for people with disabilities, families with babies, etc.) and brief the ushers accordingly;
- Arrange a stag night for the groom, preferably a few days before the wedding so that heads and stomachs have time to recover;
- Attend the ceremony rehearsal and check access, car parking, and so on;
- If the newly-weds will be going abroad for a honeymoon, remind the groom about passports, visas, currency and insurance;

- Check that buttonholes have been ordered for himself, the groom and ushers. (For convenience, these are often ordered with the bridal flowers, but it should not be taken for granted that they will be. The groom normally pays for all buttonholes, except the bride's father's);
- Check the route to the church from wherever the bride and the groom will each leave 48 to 24 hours before the wedding day. Advise the bride's father and the groom, should there be a problem, and ensure that transport arrangements are altered, if necessary;
- Arrange for umbrellas in case of rain, golf umbrellas are best because of the widespread of protection they give;
- Collect orders of service from the bride's mother, or the bride herself, a few days before the wedding;
- Make sure that the ushers can all get to the church on time. The company that is providing the bridal transport may be able to provide a car for the ushers, and the groom and best man, if they need it. Check that the bride's father will not be billed for it, the groom should pay;
- Check with the minister/priest that all is well. Do anything that needs to be done in this respect.

The wedding day

Early on the day of the wedding, the best man should:

- Check with the ushers that their outfits are complete and that they have buttonholes;
- Check with the bride's father that all is well;
- Collect his own outfit and buttonholes (if not already done) and meet the groom at his home, or the place from where he will leave for the church, a couple of hours before they need to leave;
- Check that there will be several large umbrellas available on the day and arrange for them to be easily accessible;
- Check the groom has everything he will need for the honeymoon, should the newly-weds plan to leave that day, and make sure the luggage is in the right transport, if appropriate;
- Keep the groom as calm as possible and make sure they both leave for the church, timing their arrival there for 30 to 40 minutes before the ceremony is due to begin. Let the bride's father know when they leave.

At the church the best man should:

- Make sure the ushers have arrived and give them the orders of service to hand out to arriving guests, with prayer and hymn books if appropriate;
- Pay the church fees to the minister/priest;
- Keeping an eye on the ushers, remain with the groom during the wait for the bride and stay by his side through the ceremony until the ring has been handed to the groom, then sit down in the front pew, right-hand side;
- Accompany the chief bridesmaid or matron-of-honour to the vestry, with the bride and groom and their parents, for the signing of the Register;
- Join the procession down the aisle, following the bride and groom out of the church, with the chief bridesmaid on his left arm;
- Break out umbrellas and mobilise the ushers, if it rains;
- Make sure the ushers check the church for mislaid belongings;
- Help the photographer to group guests for photographs;
- Make sure all the guests have transport to the reception, helping them to find a ride, if necessary;
- Make sure the attendants, including himself, leave the church immediately the bridal car has left with the bride and groom, with the object of arriving at the reception soon afterwards.

At the reception the best man should:

- Join the receiving line to greet arriving guests. The receiving line should begin with the bride's father and mother, then the newly-weds, the chief bridesmaid or matron-of-honour with the best man last (the groom's parents may also join the line);
- Collect any greetings messages from the bride's father and/or the hotel reception, if appropriate;
- Make sure that the bridesmaids and ushers are looking after the guests (taking coats, helping them to find their seats, and so on);
- When everyone is seated, call for silence and invite the minister/priest to say grace, or say grace himself if the minister is not present (if a buffet meal has been arranged, make sure the caterer does not start to serve until the grace has been said, even though most guests will still be standing at this time);

- After the bride's father has given his speech and offered a toast to the bridesmaids, the best man should reply to that toast, thank the bride's father on their behalf then deliver his own speech, read the congratulatory messages, and toast the newly-weds' happiness;
- After the bride and groom have opened the dancing, take the chief bridesmaid or matron-of-honour out onto the floor for the first dance;
- Throughout the reception, keep an eye on the newly-weds and rescue them if they are monopolised by any of their guests.

After the wedding

After the reception the best man should collect and return any umbrellas to their owners. On the day after the wedding he should make sure that any outfits hired for the ushers, himself or the groom are collected, so that they can be returned, and deposits collected, as soon as is practicable.

> The best man does not have to be male. Traditionally it is, of course, a male role, but it is a custom only and not written in tablets of stone. A female best 'man' is a rarity but it has happened. The most widely known example is that of non-identical twins: the young man asked his twin sister to be his best man and he returned the favour when she married his wife's brother two years later!

During the week following the wedding he should write a note to the bride and groom thanking them for their gift (*see* p77). He should also write to the bride's parents thanking them for their hospitality and groom's parents for any help and support they may have offered throughout the planning period.

The list of best man duties is a formidable one which has put many a stout-hearted young man into fear and trembling! It is really not as heavy a load as it might appear at first, especially in today's more relaxed social structure where roles are so much less rigid than they were even a few years ago. Most best men find the role less nerve wracking than they first believe it will be and enjoy the experience.

Ushers

Ushers have only a few duties to perform, but they are important because the ushers are the guest's guardians and shepherds. Their other role is to look after the bridesmaids, escorting them out of the church and at the reception which, if the bride, the groom and the best man have chosen their attendants well, should be a pleasant experience for all of them.

The ushers' duties are as follows:

Before the wedding

- Arrange and pay for the outfits they will wear at the wedding, based on guidance from the groom and best man;

The wedding day

- Arrive at the church 40 to 50 minutes before the ceremony is due to start and check-in with the best man as soon as he arrives;
- Hand out orders of service, hymn and prayer books to arriving guests and escort them to their seats, bride's family on the left (facing the altar) at the front, with her friends further back; the groom's family on the right at the front with his friends further back. The front pews should be left empty, reserved for parents and attendants. Ushers should reserve seats for themselves towards the front of the church and at the aisle end of pews so they are in a good position to join the bridesmaids as the party leaves the church at the end of the ceremony.

> The best man will know, from studying the guest list, whether the traditional seating arrangement is likely to cause an imbalance between the two groups of family and friends. Ushers should use a little discretion and, if one side of the church has significantly more guests than the other, they may like to even out the distribution a little as guests arrive.

- Help guests with parking, if the area is difficult. This should be discussed and arranged in advance with the best man;

- Escort the bridesmaids walking on their right-hand side, in procession, out of the church at the end of the ceremony, following along behind the best man and chief bridesmaid or matron-of-honour;
- Help the best man arrange guests for group photographs;
- Check that guests have left no personal possessions in the church;
- If it is raining, man the umbrellas to protect the newly-weds, bridesmaids and immediate family;
- At the reception, partner the bridesmaids in dancing and generally help them look after guests.

After the wedding

- Return their outfits, if they have been hired, as soon as is practicable;
- Send a note to the bride and groom thanking them for their gift;
- Write to the bride's parents thanking them for their hospitality.

Bride's father

The bride's father escorts his daughter to the church and gives her in marriage to her groom. A seemingly simple role, but an emotionally charged one for most fathers. He also, traditionally, pays for a large part of the wedding costs although nowadays, with more people living independently from their parents for, perhaps, several years before marriage, this responsibility tends to be shared between the bride herself, her parents, the groom and even the groom's parents.

If, for whatever reason, the bride's father cannot be present, his role may be filled by an uncle, a grandfather, an elder brother or a family friend.

Before the wedding

The bride's father's role before the wedding is quite light and includes:

- Arranging to hire or buy a suitable outfit for the wedding;
- Preparing and practising a speech;
- Being on hand with cheque book and pen.

The wedding day

On the day of the wedding the bride's father:

- Stays with the bride, when everyone else has left, and escorts her to the church;
- Escorts the bride up the aisle, walking on her right-hand side with her right hand resting on his left hand;
- When asked by the minister/priest 'Who gives this woman to be married to this man?' he replies 'I do', moves forward to the bride's side, takes her right hand in his own and places it on to the minister's outstretched hands;

The part of the service where the bride's father gives her hand to the minister/priest can be omitted, if requested. Many brides feel this is an outdated practice with no place in a modern society, even as a tradition. It should be discussed with the minister/priest well in advance of the ceremony, if necessary, as should the part of the vows that says '...to love, honour and obey...' if the bride would prefer to omit 'obey' from her vows.

- At this point, the bride's father should move away from the bride and take a seat in the front pew, left side, next to the bride's mother;
- Accompany the newly-weds, the bride's mother, best man, chief bridesmaid or matron-of-honour and groom's parents to witness the signing of the register in the vestry;
- Proceed down the aisle, following behind the bridesmaids and ushers and with the groom's mother on his left arm;
- Leave for the reception immediately after the bride and groom;
- Take second place in the receiving line, after the bride's mother, followed by the bride, the groom, the chief bridesmaid or matron-of-honour, to welcome wedding guests to the reception;
- Perform the usual duties of a host at the reception, enlisting the help of the best man, bridesmaids and ushers as necessary;
- After grace has been said, signal waiting staff to begin serving;
- After the meal, during coffee and liqueurs, and after the best man has called for silence, deliver the speech and toast the bride and groom.

Bride's mother

Arguably the busiest of all roles in wedding planning, the bride's mother, both traditionally and practically, puts a great deal of hard, but exciting, work into the months before a wedding. Most mothers enjoy every moment, even though they may spend the better part of a year alternately energised and drained by the whole thing!

On the big day itself, there is little for the bride's mother to do except enjoy the fruits of her efforts, but beforehand is quite a different matter.

Before the wedding

The bride's mother will, together with her daughter and the bride's father throughout:

- Draw up a guest list with the help of the groom's mother;

- Arrange press announcements and let family and friends know the wedding date;
- Choose and order the stationery;
- Choose and order the wedding cake;
- Choose and book a photographer and video company;
- Choose and book transport;
- Choose and book the reception venue;
- Choose and book a caterer (if the reception is to be held elsewhere than a location with catering included);
- Choose and book entertainment;
- Choose a florist and order flowers;
- Choose the menu, wine and table arrangements at the reception venue;
- Book accommodation for guests planning to stay overnight and also for the convenience of guests and the newly-weds on the wedding day (to change clothes, provide a quiet space for guests', comfort, somewhere for children to rest/be entertained) as appropriate;
- Send out invitations and monitor replies;
- Receive and store gifts, making sure that thank you notes are sent within a few days;
- Discuss personal outfits with the groom's mother, decide on what to wear to the wedding and go shopping;
- Monitor progress and chase tardy replies.

The wedding day

On the day of the wedding the bride's mother will:

- Help the bride and her attendants to get ready;
- With help from the chief bridesmaid/matron-of-honour, shield the bride from any difficulties that may arise;
- Travel to church with the bridesmaids and take her place in the front pew on the left-hand side (facing the chancel and choir) of the church;
- Accompany the newly-weds to the vestry, with the bride's father, groom's parents, best man and chief bridesmaid/matron-of honour to witness the signing of the register;
- Join the procession out of the church, following directly behind the paired attendants, on the left-hand side of the groom's father;
- Leave for the reception as soon as the photographer has finished his work outside the church;
- Join the reception line and welcome guests as they arrive;

- Be hostess at the reception and, with the help of bridesmaids and ushers, ensure that guests are well looked after throughout the day;
- With the chief bridesmaid/matron-of-honour, make sure any gifts received on the day are displayed for guests to see, make up a list of givers as the gifts are received (to help later identification in order to send thank you notes) and ensure they are taken back to the newly-weds' home or other convenient place at the end of the reception. (It may be expedient to leave them at the hotel overnight, providing management has the space and security can be guaranteed);
- Arrange for the remains of the cake to be taken home after the reception;
- Make sure everyone has left before leaving for home herself;

After the wedding

After the wedding day, the bride's mother will:

- Send pieces of the wedding cake to absent family and friends;
- Arrange to circulate proof copies of the photographs and video, and collect orders from those who want copies;
- Pass on the order, collect monies owing and send copies of the pictures to those who have ordered them as soon as they are ready.

A daughter's wedding day can be an emotional time for the whole family, but especially for her parents. Even though they feel at something of a loose end after all the hectic activity, when the excitement subsides they will be thankful to relax.

Groom's parents

Traditionally the groom's parents have little to do, since the bride's parents are hosts for the wedding and handle most of the planning. If the bride has no living parents, however, and no close relatives to fill their roles, the groom's parents may step into the breach as long as the bride is happy to accept their help and support.

They will, of course, help and support their son and, if they don't already know the bride and/or her family, they may wish to adopt a leading role in developing a friendship during the planning period.

6

COUNTDOWN

This chapter contains models for a number of lists and reminders that you might find helpful when trying to keep track of all the things that need to be done in the next few weeks and months.

The 'Countdown – nine months to Wedding Day' (*see* p111) shows an example of a wedding planned with nine months in which to do it all. The format can be adapted easily to suit any period and to reflect your own priorities.

The 'Budget Form' (*see* p114) is to remind you of the items you will, or may wish, to buy. All the standard items are listed, to help make sure nothing important is overlooked, and there are two spare spaces, marked as 'Other' at the bottom in case you want to add anything else. The 'Contingency' space is for an additional percentage to take care of the unexpected or suddenly-more-expensive-than-you-first-thought additions to the budget. If you're pretty good at working out planning budgets, you may need to add only around five per cent to the total but, if you're uncertain when it comes to looking ahead, nearer ten per cent would be wise. The Budget Form is the first shot, the means by which you can determine how much, or little, you want to spend on each item before you begin to look around for suppliers and ask for estimates. Both the Budget Form and the 'Suppliers and Costs' form will help you keep track of how close your original plan was to reality and allow you to revise your forecasts as you go along.

Next come the more specific issues, especially related to collecting information from traders and suppliers of wedding services. In requesting information it is quite important to ask each different trader for exactly the same thing. That sounds like a statement of the obvious but it is very easy to fall into agreement with someone who is trying to be helpful, by suggesting little additions and refinements that sound interesting, then find that you have collected three different quotations for three rather different things instead of the same one. The 'Quotation/Estimate Specification' record (*see* p115) is designed to help you avoid that problem.

The 'Suppliers and Costs' record keeps track of which people you've spoken too, when you contacted them and what prices they quoted. Bear in mind that price does not always reflect quality and it is a good idea to ask for a sample, or to see an example, to satisfy yourself before making a commitment.

On page 121 you will find an example of how you might fill in the Suppliers and Costs record. You might like to record details directly in this book, or you might prefer to photocopy these pages and keep them in your wedding file or folder. Keeping track of the timetable and your expenditure will help you to stay calm and relaxed, knowing that everything is under control and in hand.

Most of the quotes/estimates you collect will be actual costs; for example, when the transport company say that the bridal limousine you want to hire will cost £390, that will almost always be the actual price you will pay, even if the wedding is 12 months away. It is always a good idea to ask, and confirm the position just in case but, as a rule, that is the way the wedding market works.

It can, however, be a little misleading at times. Prices sometimes seem rather high until you remember that the quote you receive today is for a service you will receive several months in the future and, by accepting the quotation, you should be guaranteeing that there will be no price increase in the meantime. That is the main reason why it is good practice to check the basis of the supplier's quote before agreeing to it.

These models of reminders and lists are just a few of many you, and others involved in planning, could use. They are all flexible and easily adapted to suit the best man, the bride's mother and so on, according to need.

Countdown – nine months to Wedding Day (WD)

Week	To do	By whom?	Done (✓)
37	Tell parents and arrange for them to meet	B & G	
36	Make a list of everyone to tell	B, G, PB, PG	
35	Notify family and friends	B, G, PB, PG	
	Arrange press announcements	BP	
34			
33	Decide on type and style of wedding	B, G, BP	
32	Begin researching reception venues	MB, B, G	
31	Visit minister/priest/registrar to book date and gather information on costs, arrangements, etc.	B, G	
30	Write to superintendent registrar to confirm (if necessary)	B, G	
29	Begin compiling guest list	B, G, PB, PG	
28			
27			
26	Draft a rough budget of available finance	B, G, PB, PG	
25	Begin research on photographer, video, dresses, accessories, cake-makers, transport, entertainment as appropriate	B, G, MB	
24	Decide on bridesmaids and ask them	B	
23	Book honeymoon and apply for passports	G (& B)	
22			
21			
20			
19	Choose and book reception venue	B, G, PB	
	Choose and book traders/suppliers	B, PB	
18	Update draft budget based on quotes	B, PB	
17	Begin looking for bridal gown and accessories	B, MB, CB	

Week	To do	By whom?	Done (✓)
16	Choose best man and ask him	G	
	Choose church music	B, G	
15	Choose bridal gown and order	B, MB, CB	
	Choose and order stationery (if not already done)	B, MB, CB	
14	Choose and order bridesmaids dresses	B, CB, MB	
13	Choose and order/book other traders/suppliers	B, MB, G	
	Draw up gift list	B, MB, G	
12	Send out invitations	B, MB	
11	Send out gift list	B, MB	
	Visit registrar, if appropriate	B, G	
10	Choose and book florist, if not already done	B, MB	
9	Book hairdresser and beauty therapist, if home visit on wedding day is required	B, CB	
	Choose and reserve men's outfits	G, U, BM, FB, FG	
8	Arrange rehearsal	B, G	
7	Arrange wedding night accommodation	G	
6	Buy gifts for attendants	B, G	
	Brief attendants on duties	B, G	
5	Buy rings	B, G	
	Medical/health for honeymoon	B, G	
4	Dress fittings (if made to measure)	B, CB, Br	
	Choose going-away outfits	G, BM, B, CB	
3	Arrange press announcements	P, B	
	Check honeymoon tickets, etc.	G	
	Draft speeches	G, BM, FB	
2	Rehearsal (church only)	B, G, PB, PG, BM, CB, U, Br	
	Final dress fittings	B, Br, CB	
	Arrange stag/hen nights	CB, BM	
1	Stag/Hen nights	B, CB, Br	
	Check and confirm all traders/suppliers	MB, B	
	Delegate all wedding day tasks	B, G, PB	

Week	To do	By whom?	Done (✓)
1 day	Check all certificates and licences	B, G	
	Orders of service to best man (unless other arrangements made)	B	
	Dresses collected, or delivered	B, Br, CB	
	Pack for wedding night/honeymoon	B, G	
	Check transport away from reception	G	
WD	Relax	All	

Key

MB	= Mother of the Bride	B	= Bride
FB	= Father of the Bride	G	= Groom
PB	= Parents of the Bride	PG	= Parents of the Groom
CB	= Chief Bridesmaid	FG	= Father of the Groom
U	= Ushers	Br	= Bridesmaids
BM	= Best Man	M	= Minister

Budget Form

Service	Estimate	Agreed cost	Actual cost
Bridal gown			
Bridal accessories			
Bridesmaids' dresses			
Bridesmaids' accessories			
Children's outfits			
Menswear			
Rings			
Cake			
Attendants' gifts			
Stationery and postage			
Photography			
Video			
Flowers			
Balloons			
Transport			
Entertainment			
Reception (catered but ex. wine)			
Wine (with the meal and for toast)			
Funding for the bar			
Honeymoon			
Other			
Other			
Contingency			
Total			

— Quotation/Estimate Specification —

Examples

Specification – flowers

The bridal bouquet is to be made of cream gardenias and cream and red roses with ferns and ivy trailing in a pear-drop shape approximately 30 cm (12 inches) wide at its widest point and 60 cm (24 inches) at its longest.

Four bridesmaids will carry a circular posy each, approximately 15 cm (6 inches) in diameter, made of cream gardenias and deep pink carnations.

Five buttonholes: 2 x red roses and 3 x cream roses.

Photography

Twenty colour and fifteen black and white pictures to be displayed in a cream leather souvenir binder, style number 0000, (with pockets for other items).

Bridal veil

Ivory veil in fine net gathered into comb, with over face fall of 60 cm (24 inches) and back fall 2 m (6ft 6in) long (to match the train on the dress). Veil to be trimmed with Nottingham lace edging 10 cm (4 inches) wide (butterfly design).

Suppliers and Costs

For the wedding of .... and ....
on .... (date)

Service	Supplier/ trader	Date contacted	Price quoted	Accepted	Actual cost	Paid (✓)
Reception venue						
Photographer						
Video						
Florist						
Transport						

Service	Supplier/ trader	Date contacted	Price quoted	Accepted	Actual cost	Paid (✓)
Bridal gown						
Bride's shoes						
Bride's veil						
Bride's headdress						
Bride's lingerie						
Bridesmaids' dresses						

Service	Supplier/ trader	Date contacted	Price quoted	Accepted	Actual cost	Paid (✓)
Bridesmaids' shoes						
Bridesmaids' headdresses						
Attendants' gifts						
Groom's outfit						
Bride's father's outfit						
Bride's mother's outfit						

Service	Supplier/ trader	Date contacted	Price quoted	Accepted	Actual cost	Paid (✓)
Rings						
Balloons						
Stationery and postage						
Cake						
Make-up						
Hairdresser						

Service	Supplier/ trader	Date contacted	Price quoted	Accepted	Actual cost	Paid (✓)
Church/register office fees						
Entertainment						
Other						

Example

Service	Supplier/ trader	Date contacted	Price quoted	Accepted	Actual cost	Paid (✓)
Reception venue	Raven Hotel	4 Aug	£42.50	No		
	Crescent Hotel	8 Aug	£61.00	No		
	Albany Hotel	11 Aug	£53.75	Yes	£53.75 per head	✓
Photographer	You've Been Framed	16 Sept	£585.00			
	Callan Photo.	18 Sept				
	Ivan's Camera Shop					

7

THE BIG DAY

It's finally arrived, the day you've been waiting for and thought would never come. Now it's here you're nervous as a kitten and daren't look in the mirror because you didn't sleep a wink last night and you must look a wreck...! Don't panic, all the careful preparations are done, your hard work is all behind you and everything is in its place. Today is *your* day, you're the star, so enjoy yourself.

In this chapter we look at ways of organising the wedding day itself with the intention of making sure that everything runs smoothly and everyone is in the right place at the right time. It is easy to underestimate how long things take to finish, even little tasks take much longer than we often think they will. It is easy to forget something when you are busy and nervous.

On pages 144–8 we show two models you might use to help plan the day, or you can adapt them to fit your own circumstances. Whichever you decide, you will find writing it down helps to clarify your thoughts and makes it much easier to sail through the day without a hitch.

Preparation

It would be surprising if there are not a few tale-tale signs of tension around on the wedding day, which is, after all, the culmination of weeks of planning. So what can you do to minimise stress and help to ensure a happy and successful day?

Every bride looks radiant on her wedding day and careful make-up teamed with healthy, shining hair completes the picture. Any beauty therapist knows that beauty is more than skin deep and some preparation in the run up to the wedding day will help to ensure the bride is at her very best for the wedding day.

If the bride and bridesmaids will be wearing a new hairstyle and/or new make-up colours or products, a rehearsal two to three weeks before the wedding is a good idea to make sure that no-one has an undiscovered allergy or looks dreadful in the lipstick someone has recommended so highly! The make-up artist and hairdresser will suggest how much time to allow and a rehearsal will help to confirm their timetables.

Swimming and walking are both good, all-round forms of exercise that don't need expensive equipment or a punishing regime. Aerobics, both low and high impact, and step aerobics classes are held in most sports and health clubs and less commonly known activities, such as tap dancing, can be hugely enjoyable without breaking the bank or back. Exercise is, of course, most beneficial when carried out over long periods of time as long as it is geared to the individual's current state of health and fitness, even a little can go a long way.

Exercise also helps promote relaxation. So many people nowadays suffer from stress-related illnesses and arranging a wedding can certainly be stressful at times, especially if it is your own! Relaxation smooths out the skin, especially around the eyes, aids digestion and promotes a general feeling of wellbeing. It also helps to encourage sound sleep. The simplest way to relax is to put on a gentle, rhythmic sound tape (sounds of the sea and whale songs are said to be particularly effective), lie on the floor with a very shallow pillow, just to cushion the back of the head from the floor without raising it too far, in a dim, warm, draught-free room with your feet slightly raised and eyes closed. Concentrate breathing into a slow, deep rhythm centred on the diaphragm and empty the mind – wonderfully soothing.

If the ceremony is to be held in the morning, and the bride has several attendants, all of whom hope for the attention of a make-up artist and hairdresser, it might be best to avoid inviting them all to the bride's home, if space is limited. In these circumstances it may be more convenient for everyone to visit her own hairdresser/beauty studio and meet at the bride's home to change clothes and sort out any last minute details. The exception is the chief bridesmaid/matron-of-honour who should really be with the bride while she gets ready.

If there is time, and space is not a problem, there are benefits from having the bride and attendants all under the same roof as they prepare. They will be able to help each other with unfamiliar clothes (how do you run up and down stairs while wearing a long skirt with a hoop under it?) and rehearse their wedding duties together.

It is said to be bad luck for the groom to see his bride before the ceremony on the day itself. This dates back to the Dark Ages, and perhaps even earlier, when a groom with wealth and breeding spent the night before the wedding in church, on his knees, praying for the forgiveness of past sins and the strength to avoid new ones. Carnal thoughts about women would jeopardise this state of grace and, since women were temptation personified against which a mere male had no defence, their company was avoided during the period between the vigil and the wedding. The groom was often accompanied by his squire and/or a friend or two and the vigil has gradually evolved into two, separate traditions carried forward up to the present day. First, the vigil of the groom, watched over by his friends and/or servants, has evolved into the 'stag' night and secondly, the avoidance of any female company has evolved into the superstition attached to seeing the bride.

Time for herself

Looking her best on her wedding day is a top priority for every bride. If she is having a professional beauty treatment on the day, it is a good idea to plan well ahead, not just for the time it will take but for exactly what she wants to do.

Whether the bride will be alone as she prepares, or whether her attendants are with her, a warm, relaxing bath in peace and privacy should be top priority. Aromatherapy offers a number of herbal mixtures designed to promote relaxation and a small glass of wine has been known to work wonders! If the house is not too noisy, gentle music in the background can also be quite soothing.

We tend to perspire more when we are nervous and almost everyone is likely to be nervous today! Talcum powders and full-strength perfumes should be avoided because the former makes the skin prickle and irritate as it mixes with perspiration and the latter may be overpowering as skin warms up more than usual. Stick to a good, non-perfumed deodorant and a light cologne in a favourite scent.

When everyone is ready, the bride's mother and attendants leave for the church in the first car allowing father and daughter a few precious moments together before it is their turn to leave.

The Anglican ceremony

Ushers

Ushers should be the first at arrive at the church, around 30 to 40 minutes before the ceremony is take place. The best man should have made sure, in advance, that the ushers know how to seat the guests, have enough orders of service (where appropriate), and prayer and hymn books for everyone.

Seats in the front pew on the right-hand side should be reserved for the groom and his best man, with the groom's family seated alongside and immediately behind, in the second pew. The front pew on the left is reserved for the bride's parents and the bride's attendants. Guests will begin to arrive 15 to 20 minutes before the ceremony and the ushers show them to their seats. Seating the bride's family and friends on the left and the groom's family and friends on the right.

Close family of the bride and groom are seated at the front, directly behind parents and attendants, graduating to other relatives and then friends in pews further back. The best man should have checked out the local parking situation in advance and, if there is a problem, the ushers should be briefed beforehand.

Bridesmaids and bride's mother

The next to arrive are the bridesmaids and the bride's mother. The bride's mother will probably wait with the bridesmaids at the church entrance until the bride's car arrives, especially if any of the bridesmaids are very young, but she should be seated in her place, in front row on the left-hand side, before the bride actually enters the church.

> Overheard at a recent wedding, bridesmaid (bride's sister, aged six) to bride's mum: 'How will he know it's really her mummy? He's never seen her in a dress before!'

Arrival of the bride

At the bride's home, the chauffeur should escort the bride and her father to the car which should be parked so that the bride can enter and sit directly behind the front passenger seat without needing to shuffle across the rear seat or walk out into the road. This puts her on her father's left-hand side as he sits behind the chauffeur.

On arrival at the church the chauffeur pull up so that the bride can alight directly, again so that she does not need to shuffle across the seat. The chauffeur should first open the door for the bride's father to alight, then they both walk round the rear of the car and the chauffeur opens the door for the bride. Her father helps her alight and then offers her his left arm as they walk up the church path to the entrance. If it is raining the chauffeur should escort his passengers to the church entrance with an umbrella.

> Traditionally, a lady is always placed on the left-hand side of a gentleman so that, as they walk, his right hand is free to draw and use his sword in the event of trouble. How left-handed gentlemen managed is not explained!

At the church door the bridesmaids help the bride to make sure her gown, veil and headdress are neatly arranged and secure before they take their places behind her, in pairs with the youngest first, and begin their progress up the aisle.

As the bride and her father enter the church they should pause to give one of the ushers time to signal to the minister/priest that the bride is ready. At the usher's signal, the organist begins to play the music chosen for the progress and the groom and best man leave their seats to stand in front of the chancel steps, facing the minister/priest, waiting for the bride and her father to join them.

At the chancel steps

On arrival at the chancel steps the bride releases her father's arm and he moves to take up his position on her left, a small pace behind her, with the groom on her right-hand side. The best man stands on the groom's right, a small pace behind him. The bride hands her flowers, and anything else she is carrying, including gloves, to her chief bridesmaid or matron-of-honour so that her hands are free. If there are no attendants, she hands these items to her father who gives them to her mother, seated in the front pew on his left. The bridesmaids and other attendants seat themselves with the bride's mother in the front pew, left-hand side.

The minister/priest begins the ceremony with a short address, reminding the congregation of the solemnity of the occasion and that it is a happy event for the families and for the couple who are bringing them together through matrimony. Guests follow the service with their orders of service or prayer books, as appropriate.

After the minister has asked the bride and groom separately whether they will each take the other as spouse, the minister asks 'Who giveth this woman to be married to this man?' The bride's father steps forward saying 'I do', takes her right hand in his and places it, palm down, in the minister's hand. The minister then places her hand in the groom's right hand and the symbolic gesture of 'giving away' the bride is complete.

Giving away the bride is a tradition that goes back to long before the emancipation of women, to a time when a single girl belonged to her father in much the same way as did a dog or a horse. Any property or wealth she owned was her father's to control in any way he saw fit since it was widely believed that a woman's brain was incapable of dealing with matters of business and finance. In Victorian times a single woman could take control of her own property once she reached the age of 30 (although in reality many fathers never let go of the reins), at which age she also no longer needed parental consent to marry. Convention decreed, however, that permission should still be sought and the father's opinion was given great weight. On her marriage, at whatever age, her husband took over control of her property, taking over where her father, or she herself, had left off. Even if she was 30 or older, and had already experienced the responsibility of controlling her own assets, she was still bound, by law, to give control to her husband on her marriage. The present symbolic act of 'giving away the bride' had, at this time, a very real and literal meaning since marriage involved her father giving both her and her property, quite literally, into the total control of her new husband.

With prior arrangement with the minister this part of the ceremony may be omitted, and it often is nowadays, largely because, even as a tradition, it can be an emotive issue. Sometimes it is omitted because the bride has no-one to stand with her in the father's role and she prefers not to have a substitute, or if the couple are older and the words are not appropriate for their situation.

Vows and rings

The bride and groom now exchange their vows and rings. The best man places the rings on the minister's prayer book under the minister's guidance. After the exchange of vows and rings, the couple are declared husband and wife and are invited to kiss to seal the ceremony. Many congregations applaud at this point and most ministers/priests are delighted to join in.

> The ring symbolises the cycle of life, death and rebirth promised by Christ and of the never-ending nature of the marriage vows. Gold represents the indestructible nature of marriage since gold is the only natural metal that never rusts, changes or loses its sheen. The ring is placed on the third finger of the left hand because this was thought to be linked, through some form of life force, with the heart, the seat of emotion. Modern medicine, and an improved knowledge of anatomy, has disproved this belief, but the tradition continues anyway, at least in our culture. Rings worn on the right or left hand, a jewel worn in a pierced nose, head gear which hides a woman's hair and many other ways signal a woman's marital status in different cultures.

At this point the bride's father takes his seat in the front pew with the bride's mother, and the best man takes his seat in the front pew on the right-hand side of the aisle. The couple now kneel at the chancel steps to receive the blessing and, after prayers and, perhaps, a hymn, the minister/priest leads them to the altar. If there is to be a communion, it may be made at this point, or at the end of the marriage service which is concluded with prayers and a hymn as the minister/priest stands before the altar.

The newly married couple, their parents, (bride's mother first, escorted by the groom's father, then the groom's mother escorted by the bride's father) the chief bridesmaid or matron-of-honour and the best man now go into the vestry, with the minister, to sign the register. If the vestry is large enough to admit all the bride's attendants, they should also go with the group, bringing up the rear. In the vestry, the marriage certificate (a copy of the register entry) is completed and given to the couple. In the body of the church, the choir and/or organist perform for the congregation.

The bride retrieves her flowers from the chief bridesmaid or matron-of-honour and the party leaves the vestry to re-enter the body of the church.

Leaving the church

The procession forms behind the couple as they walk down the aisle. The flower girl (if there is one) walks ahead of the bride and groom scattering flower petals as she goes. After the bride and groom, the page boy and ring bearer follow together, both now carrying the train (if applicable), followed by the best man and chief bridesmaid or matron-of-honour, then ushers paired with bridesmaids. The bride's mother walks with the groom's father, and the groom's mother walks with the bride's father as they follow the attendants, with family and friends following on in turn, from the front pews first, as the procession passes.

Confetti is a modern substitute for rice, or other grain seeds, which were scattered over the bride and groom, and beneath their feet, to invoke a life of plenty and freedom from hunger, being a symbol of growth and successful harvest.

Video and photography

The general view is that flashes and clicks during the ceremony can be very distracting, for the minister as well as for everyone else, and so many of the clergy refuse permission to photograph or record the ceremony itself. Ushers should tell guests carrying cameras, as they arrive, whether they can use them in the church.

Depending on what the minister/priest has agreed both photographer and video maker should arrive at the church with plenty of time to set up for shots of the interior before the ceremony. Both should take steps to ensure that, whatever shots they take, their presence does not intrude into the service in any way.

Outside, after the ceremony the photographer arranges guests for group pictures, with the help of the ushers, and takes individual and paired shots of the bride and groom. Although guests should never leave before the bridal couple, a wet or cold day will see some begin to drift away in two's and small groups, if the photographer takes too long with his or her task. It is the best man's duty to make sure this doesn't happen.

A winter wedding can leave a bride almost blue with cold and even in summer, a thin silky dress can be decidedly chilly on a blustery day. If the bride would prefer to be somewhere warmer, she should say so. Alternatively, thermal underwear is light and very pretty nowadays, just the job for cooler days.

Since the photographic session can take some while to complete, the video maker will generally be ready to leave first, giving him or her the opportunity to set up equipment at the reception to record the bridal couple arriving.

It is a kindness to warn guests they are likely to be on video so they are not caught unawares, like one gentleman seen snoozing during the minister's address!

— Ceremonies of other churches —

The ceremonies of other Churches within the Christian faith are very similar to the one described above. For members of the Catholic Church, a wedding ceremony may be performed as a full nuptial mass just as an Anglican ceremony can include a communion. Non-conformist Church wedding ceremonies are generally simpler and the ministers are always happy to explain differences.

The Society of Friends (Quakers)

A Quaker marriage ceremony is, perhaps, the simplest of all; in fact it is a bit of a misnomer to call it a ceremony at all. The couple attend a normal meeting of the Friends, having invited guests, who may or may not be members of the Society, to witness the marriage. Anyone may stand and speak at any time and the couple stand to make their vows, the words and form of which have been agreed in advance by the Elders, when they feel the moment is right. After the vows have been exchanged they resume their seats, which are placed facing the body of the congregation, and the meeting continues. The end of the meeting is signalled, and the marriage solemnised, when two of the Elders stand and shake hands.

The marriage certificate is prepared after the meeting is officially over and before the congregation disperses. The wording is read aloud to the meeting and everyone in the congregation signs it before it is given to the couple.

There is no music at a Quaker wedding, no special clothes and only rarely is there an attendant of any kind. Rings may be exchanged, but it is not part of the ceremony, simply a personal choice by the couple themselves.

—— Other religions and faiths ——

Britain is a multicultural society, enriched by the traditions, cuisine, fashions and languages of many nations around the world. The peoples which have chosen to make their homes in these islands have brought with them their marriage customs and practices, and these co-exist alongside those of the established Christian Church in a largely tolerant society.

As long as civil laws are upheld, either in conjunction with (as in the Anglican Church) or alongside (for example, the Catholic Church) religious observance, and the practice is not considered blasphemous, any form of religious or quasi-religious ceremony is permitted.

Prior to any of these ceremonies, the civil preliminaries to obtain a Superintendent Registrar's Certificate (of No Impediment), plus a Licence when appropriate, must be fulfilled. If the respective religious community has no authorised minister (to act as registrar), the local registrar or the minister him or herself will advise accordingly, although practising members of the faith will probably know this already. If the minister is *not* authorised, he or she may still perform the religious part of the ceremony and the registrar should be asked to attend in order to perform the civil registration function. Alternatively, a separate, civil, ceremony may be held at the register office either before, or after, the religious ceremony.

Jewish ceremony

The form of the service may vary a little between Orthodox, Conservative or Reformed Churches but the core of the ceremony is, essentially, the same. The couple usually fast on the day of the wedding, repenting past sins and offering prayers for the happiness of their new life together. There must be a 'minyan' of the congregation present before a ceremony can be held (generally of at least ten adult members of the synagogue) and both men and women must wear a head covering, even those guests who are not members of the Jewish faith. The bride wears no jewellery or other decoration, not even her engagement ring.

The groom arrives with his best man, the bride's father and his own and all are escorted to the front of the synagogue where they stand close to the chuppah while waiting for the bride. The two mothers wait together at the synagogue entrance for the bride's arrival.

The chuppah is a canopy on four poles, symbolic of the Jewish nation's traditional nomadic lifestyle when tents were their only shelter. It is fragile, symbolising the weaknesses of men.

When the bride arrives, with her attendants, the groom and best man step under the chuppah and both fathers walk back to the synagogue entrance to greet her. On her father's left arm, the bride walks to the chuppah with her attendants following and, behind them, the groom's parents and her mother.

The couple stand underneath the chuppah which is made of silk or velvet and generally decorated with fresh flowers. The attendants gather around the couple in places agreed previously with the rabbi; which will vary according to the number of attendants there are altogether.

The rabbi, welcomes the congregation and offers a blessing. The ring is first placed on the index finger of the bride's right hand as the groom makes his vows, she is not required to make any response, her silence signifies that she accepts his vow and echoes it herself. Once this part of the ceremony is complete, the ring may be transfered to her third finger, left hand in keeping with British tradition.

The *ketuba*, or marriage document, is read aloud to the congregation and the Seven Benedictions are sung. Now the bride and groom drink from the same glass of wine, which symbolises that they will share everything in life from then on.

The glass is smashed and the groom crushes it into the ground, symbolising the exclusive nature of the marriage bond, the fragility of life, the ever-present threat of destruction and the sharing of both good and bad times. The kebuta is signed, after which the couple receive the rabbi's blessing. After the psalm of praise, the civil register is signed and the ceremony is complete.

Buddhist ceremony

Chanting forms a large part of a Buddhist wedding ceremony. As guests arrive they are greeted with chanting which continues as the groom arrives and as the congregation waits for the bride.

When she arrives, she is escorted by a lay reader to kneel, with her groom, in front of a cabinet which contains the sacred scroll. After chanting ceremonial sutras, the couple sip from three bowls of three different sizes, symbolising how their lives will grow inside their marriage.

There may be an exchange of rings, after which the lay reader delivers an address, and the ceremony concludes with guests applauding and with congratulations to the newly-weds. The register will normally be signed at this point, unless the civil ceremony is held separately elsewhere.

Hindu ceremony

Hindu wedding celebrations last a whole day, rather like a Christian wedding and reception all rolled into one. It is relatively informal in structure, being very sociable with guests moving around and talking with each other. The bride's family erect a canopy of richly patterned, heavy fabric, surrounded and decorated with flowers, under which the bride and groom exchange their vows. This place is blessed to make it sacred and holy because weddings may not always be held in a temple, especially if there are many guests.

The bride arrives first and hides somewhere close by until all the guests, and her groom, have arrived. When he arrives, he is greeted by waving lights and a shower of rice, symbolising riches and fertility. As he takes his place under the canopy, the bride's relatives bring her out of 'hiding' to join him.

After a ceremony of prayer and blessing, during which guests continue to socialise, the celebrations continue for many hours.

Muslim ceremony

An Islamic wedding is a contract, not a sacrament, having more in common with a British civil ceremony than a church wedding. The ceremony is conducted by an imam in a mosque.

Traditionally, a Muslim male is permitted to marry either a Muslim, Christian or Jewish woman but a Muslim female may marry only a Muslim male. Although there is a little more tolerance nowadays, Muslim parents still hope and expect that their daughters will marry within the faith.

The women gather on one side of the mosque, with the men on the other. The ceremony opens with a reading from the Koran, the holy book of Islam, after which the bride and groom both signify that they consent to the marriage. The imam delivers another address, which is followed by prayers and a distribution of dried fruits, such as dates and figs, to symbolise fertility and prosperity.

After the ceremony the bride's parents will host a reception at their home, at which the groom's family are guests of honour, and a week later the groom's family does the same in return.

Register office ceremony

If the wedding is held at a register office, the ceremony will be much shorter than that in a church, but it can, and should, be just as meaningful and special. Many register office brides feel it inappropriate to wear a traditional wedding gown, or have attendants and music and so on, but this is a matter of custom, rather than because of any restrictions placed on registrars, their offices or those choosing to marry there.

It is true that many register offices are less than beautiful to look at but churches, too, can often seem cold and unfriendly, especially on a winter's day when the heating system shows all its inadequacies! Nevertheless, most offices are pleasant places and staff will generally be warm and welcoming.

Before the ceremony

Preparations for the day will follow the same sort of pattern as for a church wedding but the ceremony itself is rather different. Generally, a register office wedding tends to be smaller, and more relaxed, than the church equivalent and it is likely that there will be few attendants, perhaps only one each for the bride and groom. Alternatively, the bride and groom may travel to the register office together, although the superstitious may find this quite beyond the pale!

Even though there may be no attendants to whom tasks can be delegated, someone will still need to make sure that the cake is safely at the reception, along with any gifts that are to be displayed, that flowers are delivered to the right place in plenty of time, and so on. Without the several pairs of willing hands normally supplied by attendants, the bride and her parents will need to find other ways of ensuring that last-minute tasks are completed properly, perhaps by pressing the bride's siblings into service (if she has them) or co-opting close friends.

Register offices have waiting areas where guests gather until it is time for the ceremony to begin. Since the ceremony is short, and register offices are sometimes quite busy, there may very well be two or more waiting areas, so that different bridal parties don't inconvenience each other. The way out of the office is often separated from the entrance for the same reason.

The ceremony

When the bride arrives, whether she is alone, or with members of her family or friends, she can usually expect a warm welcome from the guests already congregated, often with hugs and kisses all round, something not possible in the more formal atmosphere of a church. The groom may also be there or he may already have been ushered into the marriage room to await her arrival.

The registrar's assistant will let everyone know when it is time to go through to the marriage room. The bride should wait a moment or two, then enter the room by herself, or on the arm of her father or appointed friend, and walk to the registrar's table where the groom awaits her. The room will not have an aisle, or altar, but the bride will walk through the centre, or down the side, of rows of seats occupied by her guests.

The registrar begins by welcoming the guests and saying a few words about the ceremony before asking the couple to exchange their vows and rings. When the short ceremony is over the newly-weds are invited to be seated while the Registrar supervises the signing of the register and copies the entry on to the marriage certificate which is given to the couple.

Photography and video

Registrars have the same concerns about photography and video recordings in the marriage room as ministers do for inside a church. Even though there are no religious considerations here, flash guns and the sound of cameras can be distracting, so someone, preferably the best man, should be asked to tell guests carrying cameras whether there are restrictions on use. This is best done while guests are in the waiting area, before being shown into the marriage room.

Outside the office after the ceremony, there will be photographs and so on, exactly the same as at a church wedding. There is, however, a stronger possibility that a second location will be needed for photographs because many register offices open directly on to the street.

Second marriages

If the bride, or groom, or both, are marrying for the second time, there may very well be significant differences in how preparations, and the ceremony itself, are arranged.

For example, it is more likely that the bride and groom will have made all the arrangements and are paying for everything. Children from the couple's previous relationships may be present at the ceremony and there may be far less involvement from the couple's own parents, or even none at all.

Whatever arrangements the couple wish to make, whether for a small ceremony with only witnesses present, or an extravagant day's celebrations on a par with the classic formal church wedding, the choice is wide and entirely up to them.

The reception

Just in case some of the guests arrive at the reception early, the catering supervisor, hotel manager or the wedding arranger (if applicable) should be briefed to look after them, making sure they are made comfortable until the bridal couple arrive.

When they arrive, the bridal party forms a reception line just inside the entrance to the reception room. First is the bride's father, then the bride's mother followed by the groom's father and mother, then the bride and groom and, lastly the chief bridesmaid/matron-of-honour and best man. They welcome their guests individually.

Nowadays many receptions are less formal and it is not uncommon to dispense with the reception line altogether, with the bride and groom simply moving around the room, greeting their guests as they go.

The room where the meal is to be served should be dressed and ready before anyone arrives. Whichever method has been adopted for helping guests to find their places, ushers and bridesmaids should gradually begin to steer people towards tables, and help them as necessary, around 10 to 15 minutes after the last guest has been received and the reception line dispersed. Try to mix members of both families together as much as possible and place single guests near each other.

Speeches

When the meal is over it is time for speeches. Making a speech can be a daunting prospect for those not used to public speaking, but a sense of humour helps to keep it all in proportion. Essentially the speakers say 'thank you' and entertain a little with amusing recollections. Speeches need not be lengthy and the prospect should not be allowed to spoil the day by causing attacks of nerves. Successful speech-making is just a case of plenty of preparation, lots of practice in front of the mirror and not too much 'Dutch courage' beforehand. Construction is easy: a speech, like every good story, needs a beginning, a middle and an end. (For more advice on speech-making, consult *Speaking on Special Occasions* in the *Teach Yourself* series.)

Father of the bride's speech

First it is the turn of the bride's father. The best man attracts the attention of guests (from the top table), as soon as dessert has been cleared, asks for silence and introduces the bride's father, or the person who has assumed his role for the day. (If there is a Master of Ceremonies, he or she will perform this task.) The bride's father rises to deliver his speech which, traditionally, is full of praise for his daughter. He may tell one or two amusing and complimentary stories about her childhood and adolescence and welcome his new son-in-law into the family. He may also offer a word or two of advice on married life, in humorous vein, of course, and end his speech by proposing a toast to the bride and groom to which everyone, except the bridal couple, stand and respond.

While he has been speaking, waiting staff have been silently touring the room replenishing glasses, or serving Champagne, for the toast and serving coffee.

Groom's speech

A moment or two after the bride's father has resumed his seat, the groom rises to respond with a speech of his own. He thanks his new father-in-law for the toast and then both his new in-laws for bringing up their daughter so well and providing him with such a beautiful bride. He may thank his own parents for their love and support and, if he has any amusing anecdotes to tell, about how he and his bride met for example, or some other aspect of their life so far, he may wish to add one or two here. He closes with thanks to his best man, the bridesmaids and anyone else who has helped to make the day successful. If the attendants' gifts have not been given already he should present them now, ending his speech with a toast to the bridesmaids.

Best man's speech

The best man responds to the groom's toast and thanks him on behalf of the bridesmaids. His own speech can be much less formal than that of the bride's father or the bridegroom. They've said all the thank yous that are necessary and it is up to him now to entertain the guests. His speech should aim to be witty and amusing. Anecdotes about the groom's schooldays and adolescent misdemeanours always go down well, especially when there is a little shared history between the groom, best man and some of the guests. He should be diplomatic, however, and steer clear of anything that might embarrass the groom unnecessarily or risk upsetting the bride. He ends his speech with a toast, complimentary to the bride, with congratulations to the groom on his good fortune, and for their joint future happiness.

Cutting the cake

The last part of the ceremony is cutting the cake. After the speeches the best man (or Master of Ceremonies, if there is one) announces that the bride and groom are to cut the cake. The couple leave their seats and, together, hold the knife over the cake and make the first symbolic cut, to the accompaniment of popping camera flashes and much congratulation. The cake is taken away to be cut into serving-sized pieces. If preferred, the cake may be cut before the meal. In this case, pieces of the cake may be distributed with coffee, while the guests are listening to the speeches.

While catering staff cut up the cake, guests leave their tables and will either move to another room, gather around the bar or, if this is a summer wedding and the facilities are available, go out on to a terrace or garden. As soon as the cake has been cut, waiting staff and/or the bridesmaids hand round pieces. Since the pieces will dry out if they are not eaten, only cut sufficient for those guests present.

If the cake is large enough, the top tier may be saved for later. Traditionally, it is earmarked for the first wedding anniversary or even the first christening. A well-made cake will keep for quite a long time, as long as it is properly stored. The icing may discolour a little over time, but it can be removed and replaced as long as the cake is still good.

It is said that, if a bridesmaid sleeps with a piece of wedding cake under her pillows, she will dream of the man she will marry.

Continuing the party

If there is to be further celebration, music will bridge the gap between the wedding breakfast and any entertainment that has been arranged. If there is a disco, the DJ may begin the programme right away, or perhaps a pianist or harpist or other soloist could provide some background music while guests stretch their legs and socialise together. Some guests prefer to seek a little fresh air, take children somewhere where they can safely let off steam for a while or generally freshen up ready for the evening.

Entertainment will have been arranged already during the planning stage of wedding arrangements and it is now time for everyone, including the newly-weds and their parents, to relax, perhaps for the first time in the day.

Leaving

At some point the bride and groom may want to change out of their wedding outfits, either just to relax a little or because it is time for them to leave. The bride's mother or the best man and the chief bridesmaid/matron-of-honour will have made sure that a change of clothes and a suitable place to change has been arranged. Any hired clothing will be left in their care to be returned to the owners as soon as possible.

When it is time for the bride and groom to leave, all the guests gather to see them off. The bride's last act, before she leaves, is to throw her bouquet into the crowd. It is said that the person who catches it will be the next to marry.

Originally, the custom of catching the bride's bouquet related to only the unmarried girls and woman at the wedding, but nowadays everyone joins in.

Alone at last

Whether the couple are leaving for their honeymoon right away, staying in a hotel overnight or going home, the next few hours or even, perhaps, days will probably feel a little strange. The weeks and days leading up to the wedding day itself have been full of preparation, excitement and, quite probably, a few difficulties to resolve. Now it is over and the adrenaline rush subsides.

The wedding is not, however, the end of anything – is a beginning, the beginning of a new life which is different from the one that went before, even for couples who have lived together before marriage. At the end of the wedding day, however, the only concern of most couples is to leave the crowd behind, find some privacy and peace after the hubbub, and concentrate on each other.

In some cultures it was the custom that when a girl married, she left her parents' house to live with her husband's family, not independently but as a very junior member of an extended family group that could stretch into four generations. Her status in the family improved as she grew older, bore healthy children (especially boys) and as older members of the family died, making way for others on the hierarchical ladder. In such a society boy children were highly prized because they stayed with their parents, in the extended family group, all their lives and brought home the income that allowed their parents to live in comfort as they grew old. The boy also brought home his bride, on whose shoulders fell the task of raising her own children and, in time, caring for her elderly parents-in-law. The parents of girls had no-one to care for them in their old age, a real dilemma in the absence of any welfare state.

——— Wedding day timetables ———

The following tables models of typical wedding day programmes, one for a Church wedding and one for a register office wedding. You might like to adapt these to your own circumstances and use them as a diary-cum-reminder. By the time you reach the stage of actually working out what you will be doing on 'The Day' you will probably be feeling excited, nervous and wondering how you could ever have thought that you were different from everyone else in believing that arranging your wedding would be easy!

Many brides have gone down this path before you and have survived to enjoy and celebrate their wedding days so don't worry, you're nearly there and there's not long to wait now.

Wedding day timetable – church wedding

Ceremony due to begin at 2.30 p.m.

Where	What	When
Bride's home	The bride, her parents and attendants are preparing for the ceremony	10.30 a.m.
	Flowers arrive	
Best man's home	Best man is preparing for the ceremony	11.30 a.m.
Bride's home	Bride's mother rings reception venue to check everything OK	12.00 p.m.
	Best man arrives to collect buttonholes for himself, groom and ushers	12.15 p.m.
Groom's home	Groom and his parents are preparing for the ceremony	12.30 p.m.
Ushers' homes	Ushers are preparing for the ceremony	
Groom's home	Best man arrives	1.00 p.m.
Church	Ushers arrive and prepare prayer and hymn books/orders of service, check out seating and parking	1.45 p.m.
Bride's home	Limousine(s) arrives	1.50 p.m.
Groom's home	Best man calls bride's father to let him know he and groom are leaving for the church	1.55 p.m.

Where	What	When
Church	Groom and best man arrive: buttonholes and orders of service given to ushers	2.00 p.m.
	Guests begin to arrive, ushers give them orders of service/books, escort to seats and warn guests of camera/confetti restrictions	2.10 p.m.
	Best man finds minister and pays church fees	
Bride's home	Bride's mother and attendants leave for the church	2.15 p.m.
	Bride and father leave for church	2.20 p.m.
Church	Bride's mother and attendants arrive	2.25 p.m.
	Bells begin, choir enters the church	
	Bride and father arrive, groom and best man move into position, bride and father, with attendants, progress up aisle	2.30 p.m.
	Ceremony begins	
	Progress out of church, photo. session outside	3.20 p.m.
	Bride and groom leave for reception	3.45 p.m.
	Parents, attendants and guests leave for reception	3.50 p.m.
Reception	Parents, best man and chief bridesmaid arrive, reception line forms	3.55 p.m.
	Newly-weds arrive	4.00 p.m.
	Guests arrive and are welcomed	4.05 p.m.
	Meal is served	4.35 p.m.
	Speeches	5.15 p.m.
	Cake-cutting	5.40 p.m.
	Party/Dancing begins	6.00 p.m.

Where	What	When
	Bride and groom leave	10.30 p.m.
	Guests and attendants begin to leave	10.45 p.m.
	Reception ends; best man and chief bridesmaid take care of any clothes left by the bride and groom, and repack wedding gifts for journey to newly-wed's/ parent's home, bride's parents check reception area for lost property, etc. and thank staff	11.00 p.m.
	Bride's parents, best man and chief bridesmaid leave	11.20 p.m.

Wedding day timetable – register office

Ceremony due to begin at 11.15 a.m.

Where	What	When
Bride's home	Bride, her parents and matron-of-honour are preparing for the ceremony	8.15 a.m.
	Flowers arrive	
Best man's home	Best man is preparing for the ceremony	9.30 a.m.
Bride's home	Bride's mother rings reception venue to check everything OK	9.45 a.m.
	Best man arrives to collect buttonholes for himself and groom	9.50 a.m.
Groom's home	Groom and his parents are preparing for the ceremony	
	Best man arrives	10.00 a.m.
Bride's home	Limousine(s) arrives	10.35 a.m.
Groom's home	Best man calls bride's father to let him know he and groom are leaving for the register office	10.45 a.m.
Bride's home	Bride's mother and attendant leave	10.55 a.m.
Register Office	Groom and best man arrive	11.00 a.m.
	Guests begin to arrive	
	Bride and father arrive	11.15 a.m.
	Groom, best man and guests ushered into marriage room by registrar's assistant	11.15 a.m.
	Bride enters marriage room, ceremony commences	
	After ceremony, photo. session	11.30 a.m.

Where	What	When
Reception	Newly-weds leave for reception	11.50 a.m.
	Parents, attendants and guests leave for reception	11.55 a.m.
	Parents, best man and matron-of-honour arrive, reception line forms	12.05 p.m.
	Newly-weds arrive	12.10 p.m.
	Guests arrive and are welcomed	12.15 p.m.
	Meal is served	12.45 p.m.
	Speeches	1.30 p.m.
	Cake-cutting	1.55 p.m.
	Party/dancing begins	2.30 p.m.
	Finger buffet set out by caterer	7.00 p.m.
	Bride and groom leave	9.30 p.m.
	Guests and attendants begin to leave	10.30 p.m.
	Reception ends; best man and matron-of-honour take care of any clothes left by the bride and groom, and repack wedding gifts for journey to newly-wed's/parent's home; bride's parents check reception area for lost property, etc. and thank staff	10.50 p.m.
	Last person leaves	11.00 p.m.

8

AFTER THE
WEDDING

Americans have a saying 'the game isn't over 'til the fat lady sings' which is a reference to the end of a baseball game when an operatic diva sings the US national anthem before the crowd disperses to go home. You may not have an operatic diva at your beck and call, but there are still several things that need attention after the wedding day before it can be said that the 'game' is over.

Saying 'thank you'

Thank you is such a small thing to say, but the effect it has on the recipient far outways the small effort needed to say it. The bride's parents are the first on the list for thanks because, even in these days of less-rigid etiquette, when many other people lend a hand, most of the burden of planning and expense generally falls on them.

A week or so after the newly-weds return from honeymoon, when dust has settled, they may like to consider ways of showing their appreciation to the bride's parents. There are lots of ways to say thank you; a pair of theatre tickets, a day out, dinner at their favourite restaurant or, perhaps, the bridal bouquet, dried, pressed and mounted, as a gift would be appropriate.

The best man and other attendants have already received a small gift from the bride and groom to thank them for everything they have done but a short note, or a card, when they return from their honeymoon will round things off nicely.

The groom's parents may also warrant a thank you, especially if they have done more than generally expected to encourage and support their son throughout the planning stages. As with the bride's parents, theatre tickets, dinner at a favourite restaurant or a day out somewhere should be well received.

The less obvious recipients of thanks include the minister/priest or registrar who officiated at the ceremony, with a special mention for the organist, choir and bellringer's leaders, if appropriate, and the hotel staff or caterers who looked after the reception. People such as the cake-maker, florist, and chauffeur will all value being remembered with thanks.

Others to receive a handwritten thank you note are those who sent or brought a gift for the newly-weds. Gifts which were received before the wedding should have been acknowledged as soon as they arrived and those which arrived at the reception, or since, should be acknowledged as soon as possible afterwards.

Clearing up

Hired outfits should have been returned to the hiring company by the chief bridesmaid/matron-of-honour, the best man or whoever the task has been delegated to by the bride and groom. This messenger should also have collected any deposits and returned them to whoever paid them, but the newly-weds might like to check, just to be sure.

Most hotel function co-ordinators and hall managers will contact clients to tell them if any lost property was found when the room was cleared after a wedding reception, but, again, a phone call to check is always worthwhile.

If a complete tier of the wedding cake is still intact now is the time to store it for a future occasion if you wish. If it is to be stored, find a close-fitting, empty, cake or biscuit box, or an airtight polythene storage box, making sure it is scrupulously clean and perfectly dry. Line with layers of greaseproof paper and place the cake inside. Remove any decorations and ribbons or flowers, layer more paper around, and on top of the cake, fit the lid and store the box somewhere cool and completely free from condensation or damp of any kind.

A well-made fruit cake should keep for a very long time, in the right conditions, although the icing may discolour a little and the cake may not be quite as moist as when it was new. This can be corrected by taking off the old icing, adding some moisture (a little brandy, perhaps) and re-icing.

> An interesting story tells of a couple who contacted the bakery where their wedding cake was made, asking if they could replace slightly discoloured icing on the top tier of their wedding cake so they could use it at the baptism of their first child. It was only later that the staff at the bakery discovered it was to be an adult baptism and the child was, in fact, 17 years old! Apparently the cake was delicious!

— Photograph and video selection —

The photographer and video maker should have the results of their work ready for the couple to look at when they arrive back from their honeymoon. The couple will be able to choose a selection from the photographs, for inclusion in the wedding album.

It is not obligatory to buy an album offered by the photographer, even if his price already includes the album, and there are many designs and types of book available at any good photographic retailers. Some albums are designed as complete record books, having pages on which to record the guest list, gifts received, and so on. However, part of the photographer's profit comes from the onward sale of albums so he or she is unlikely to give much of a discount should the couple decide to buy their album elsewhere. Photographs not included in the album also belong to the newly-weds and the photographer should provide one copy of each of these.

Copyright laws almost certainly apply to the video as well as to photographs but this is unlikely to cause any real problems since wedding videos generally appeal only to those most closely involved with the bride and groom, so fewer copies are needed.

—— Flower and dress preservation ——

Wedding services directories in magazines, *Yellow Pages* and craft fairs are all good sources of craftspeople who do this sort of work. For flower preservation, the flowers will need to be looked after very well on the wedding day, preferably sprayed with clear water as soon as the bride arrives at the reception and stored somewhere very cool during the celebrations and, if necessary, overnight.

They should be delivered to the company or person engaged to do the work as quickly as possible, which means someone should be delegated to deliver them in the bride's absence. Some people working in this field operate a mail order service, in which case they will advise on how to deliver the flowers to them in good condition. Check with the company concerned well in advance. Drying can take several weeks, so don't expect instant results.

There are fewer companies specialising in the preservation of wedding dresses. If *Yellow Pages* has no listing, bridal magazines should be able to help. Some companies supply a box made specially for the purpose and a set of instructions on how to store the dress: others will ask for the dress to be delivered to them and will return it wrapped and packed ready for storage.

Every wedding dress will eventually deteriorate if stored incorrectly, and, once discolouration has occurred, it is impossible to remove. After the wedding, the dress should be expertly cleaned, hung in the fresh air for an hour or so to let every remaining trace of dry cleaning fluid evaporate, then placed inside a natural cotton bag which is long enough to take the full length of the dress without creases.

If possible, the dress should be stored flat, inside the cotton bag, but if this is not possible, it may be hung from a well-padded hanger somewhere high enough to prevent it trailing on the floor and with enough space so that it is not crushed. Stored this way, most dresses will be perfectly all right for several months but a more permanent home will be needed eventually, even if only to release much-needed wardrobe space.

Complaints

If there is any cause to complain either to, or about, any of the traders who supplied services to the wedding, now is the time to do it. If it is an item covered under the wedding insurance package, complete and send off a claim as soon as possible.

If the nature of the complaint puts it outside the terms of insurance cover, a complaint to the trader concerned should always be in writing stating clearly the nature of the problem, what happened, what was done (if anything) to try to put it right at the time and what the company is expected to do about it now.

Getting back any money paid, or an amount in compensation, is almost always difficult but, if the case is a good one, it should be possible to pursue it through the Small Claims Court at the local county court. Neighbourhood advice centres, Citizen's Advice Bureaux or the county court office, all listed in the telephone directory, will be able to advise on how to go about this.

Hopefully, your wedding will have gone without a hitch and there were no clouds on the horizon all day long. Most wedding pass without any difficulties at all but, if there is a problem, it's far more likely to be the sort of incident that ends in the collection of amusing family anecdotes than anything really serious.

Even so, if something has gone wrong and you decide to do something about it rather than just putting it down to experience, it's best done fairly soon after the wedding since the passage of time only makes it more difficult and less convincing.

9

YOUR FUTURE

The big difference between moving in with someone and marrying them is commitment, commitment that allows and encourages a long-term view and planning for a future that two people will share. Being newly married is the perfect opportunity for reviewing existing plans and making new ones. In this chapter we look at a few of the issues which are often uppermost in the minds of newly-weds and consider what they may mean to you.

Financial planning

Many people sail through life without any help at all from the people who are now called financial planners, or consultants, and manage very well. Nevertheless, there are situations where expert help and advice is useful and, occasionally, essential.

Buying a home, taking out a loan, planning a pension, insuring a life and investing in stocks and shares are just a few of the many financial issues with which people become involved. The list is long, including endowments for children's education fees, insurance for personal accident and motor cover, self-employment, business planning, and so on.

Personal financial planning can take some of the chance elements out of life, providing a fall-back position in the event of illness or accident, ensure a comfortable retirement and take care of dependants in the event of death. Traditionally, these plans have been male preserves, mostly because women have been unlikely to have the income on which planning depends. Nowadays, however, more and more women have their own incomes and more and more households are dependant on two incomes in order to maintain a desired lifestyle. Who should plan for what, and when, are the two key factors that planners are equipped to identify.

There are two entirely different types of financial planners, and the difference is crucial to those in the market place for the first time. First, are the tied agents who work as employees or agents of specific companies. They are able to compare the products which their own company markets with those of other, similar, companies but, apart from pension advice, they are not obliged to give impartial advice on which is best for a specific client. They are bound, by their contracts of employment, always to present and recommend the products of their own company, but are also obliged to explain this to potential clients at the outset of discussions.

Independent advisers are able to research different companies in the field to find the product that best suits their clients' needs, with no bias to any specific company. They will then advise which company and which product will satisfy the clients' needs best.

There are advantages and drawbacks to each. For example, the tied employee or agent has a vested interest in securing as much of your business as possible for his or her employers because his or her income, and perhaps job, rests on continuing success.

For the independent, who still relies on clients and business volume for his/her income, there is more freedom to manoeuvre because commission will be earned from whichever company receives the business he or she writes. Even here, however, there may well be constraints on impartiality because some companies pay more commission than others.

As a client, the potential buyer of services, deciding which company to use can be a thought-provoking decision but it need not be difficult. Buying financial advice is not much different from buying any other product – be clear about what you want, ask the relevant questions, listen carefully to the answers and buy what suits you best.

Gender issues

Marriage today is a rather different institution from even just a few years ago and much different from those marriages on which our parents embarked. Even so, in spite of all the challenges to gender roles which have been addressed in the past few years, some of the traditional attitudes remain.

Social studies continually show that it is the female partner who carries the greater part of the burden of childcare and homemaking in the majority of marriages and partnerships and, where there are children, the death or incapacity of the wife/mother can have a far greater financial impact on the family than the absence or incapacity of the husband/father.

It follows, therefore, that any financial planning for the family should include provision for the female partner in at least the same measure as for the male and, perhaps, even more.

—————————— Making a will ——————————

Making a will is almost universally seen as being a morbid task which only 'older' people need to worry about. Nothing could be further than from the truth. It is an act of love and caring, undertaken by those who wish to spare their loved ones the added pain of worry and, perhaps, hardship when they die, especially if that death is premature and unexpected.

Everyone has an 'estate', the term given to property, goods and money left behind by the deceased. It may be property and wealth amounting to millions of pounds, or a modest home, car and a few personal possessions. Without a will, it can be months, and sometimes years, before those left behind are able to gain access to the bank account that paid the bills, the savings that were to pay for a holiday or even the insurance money that was to pay the mortgage.

Making a will is, for most people, a simple thing to do, involving a few minutes with a solicitor or a professional will writer. In most cases costs are modest and the will is ready within a few days. Once completed, it can be tucked away somewhere safe and will be needed again on only a few occasions when circumstances suggest an updating would be advisable, such as on the birth of a child or a substantial change of financial worth – for example, hitting the jackpot on the National Lottery!

Marriage automatically invalidates any will made earlier. This will be of particular relevance and importance to people marrying later in life or those entering a second or subsequent marriage. They may have existing responsibilities, acquired before the marriage, which need to be discharged and protected after their death and making a will ensures that their wishes are carried out promptly and without confusion.

Changing a name

The majority of married women change their last name to that of their husband on marriage without realising that, although this is the custom and practice, it is not obligatory in the United Kingdom. A married woman is entitled to use either her own name, or that of her husband, or a mixture of both, as she wishes.

Last names can be changed by deed poll, as well as by marriage, but, in law, a person has the right to use, and be known by, any last name they please providing there is no intent to deceive or defraud. This means that a signature on a legally binding agreement, such as a mortgage or passport application, must be the name at birth, the name adopted on marriage or by deed poll, of the person to whom it relates.

If a married woman retains her name after marriage, she may finds it creates confusion at times, especially when travelling abroad. She may wish to carry a copy of her marriage certificate at such times.

Against this inconvenience, a married woman will often need to balance the advantages of keeping her own name. If she has already built, or is building, a flourishing career, a change of name can have serious effects where her reputation is linked with her name but where she is not, personally, known. In large organisations, where reputations travel ahead of the face, this could be a significant problem.

First names are different. One must, in law, always use the first name registered at birth, unless the whole name is changed by deed poll.

Finale

Contrary to much popular opinion, a wedding isn't the end of anything (except, perhaps, wedding planning!) but a new beginning, and everything new involves changes and adjustments. Mostly, these first few months after marriage are a time of discovery and revelation as you get to know each other and sort out your priorities.

Financial planning, property and all the other big decisions, don't need to be addressed right away, in fact they are probably best left for a while until you are more comfortable with each other.

We hope you have found this book helpful and informative, and perhaps you will recommend it to friends when it is their turn to marry: perhaps you will put it with your wedding album as a keepsake and show it to your own children when it is their turn to marry – it may be a source of great amusement twenty years from now! Whatever your plans, we wish you good luck for your future together and may your married life be prosperous and happy.

APPENDIX

—————— Useful addresses ——————

Copies of birth and/or adoption certificates and death certificates may be obtained from:

The Registrar General for England and Wales
Office of Population, Census' and Surveys
St Catherine's House
10 Kingsway
London WC2B 6JP
Tel: 0171 242 0262

General Register Office for Northern Ireland
Oxford House
49–55 Chichester Street
Belfast BT1 4HL
Tel: 01232 235211

General Register Office for Scotland
New Register House
Edinburgh EH1 3YT
Tel: 0131 334 0380

General Register Office for the Isle of Man
Finch Road
Douglas
Isle of Man
Tel: 01624 5212

Register General for Guernsey
The Greffe
Royal Court House
St Peter Port
Guernsey
Tel: 01481 725277

Sample gift list

Kitchen

Set of pans	Cooker
Cooking utensils	Refrigerator
Wooden spoons	Washing machine
Spices and a rack	Freezer
Bread bin	Dryer
Bread board	Clothes horse
Chopping board	Iron
Cheese board	Ironing board
Carving set	Washing basket
Rolling pin	Pastry board
Meat carving dish	Linen basket
Oven dishes	Buckets
Tea towels	Mop
Dusters	Broom
Oven gloves	Vacuum cleaner
Food processor	Toaster
Electric deep fat fryer	Filter coffee maker/cafetiere
Storage jars	Mixing bowls
Pudding bowls	Waste bin

Dining room

Dinner service
White wine glasses
Brandy balloons
Champagne flutes
Whisky glasses
Dining set
Tea service
Canteen of cutlery
Napkins
Cookery books
Portable television
Fire blanket
Torch

Water jug and glasses
Claret glasses
Sherry glasses
Liqueur glasses
Decanters
Dresser
Tea trays
Table cloths
Cruet set
Wok
Radio
Fire extinguisher

Bedroom

Duvet
Duvet covers
Pillows
Sheets
Pillow cases
Dressing table
Bed
Bed spread
Hairdryer

Dressing table set
Coat hangers
Bedside lamps
Alarm clock
Teasmade
Wardrobes
Blankets
Portable television

Bathroom

Bathroom mat set

Linen basket

Lounge

Suite of furniture
Book shelves
Television
Music centre
Coasters (to protect tables)

Occasional table(s)
Scatter cushions
Video
Magazine rack
Lamps

General

Towels
Waste bins
Telephone(s)
Lamp shades
Smoke alarm(s)

Vases
Pictures
Sewing machine
Set of luggage
Humidifier

Garden/garage

Lawn mower
Fork(s)
Rake
Short-handed shears
Secateurs
Trowel
Garden furniture set
Electric drill
Workmate
Papering table
Papering brush
Vehicle jump start leads
Lamp (battery attach)
Socket set
Tyre pressure gauge
Picnic basket
Do-it-yourself manual

Spade(s)
Shovel
Hoe
Long-handled shears
Hedge clippers
Dibbers
Ladder
Tool kit (screw drivers,
    hammers, etc.)
Paint brushes
Pasting brushes
Buckets
Foot (air) pump
Torch/lantern
First aid kit
Picnic table and chairs
Car rugs

INDEX